BIG RED

How I Learned Simplicity from a Suitcase

BIG RED

How I Learned Simplicity from a Suitcase

by

Ellie Dias

Buddhapuss Ink LLC

Edison NJ

Published in the United States by Buddhapuss Ink LLC, Edison, New Jersey. All rights are reserved. No part of this book may be used or reproduced in any manner whatsoever without written permission of the author except in the case of brief quotations embodied in critical articles and reviews.

Cover Photo by Robert Charles Photography
Cover and Book Layout/Design by The Book Team
Editor, MaryChris Bradley
Copyeditor, Andrea H. Curley
ISBN 978-1-941523-06-3 (Original Paperback)
First Edition April 2017
Library of Congress Control Number: 2016963028

PUBLISHER'S NOTE

Buddhapuss Ink and our logos are trademarks of Buddhapuss Ink LLC.
www.buddhapussink.com

Contact the author at:
Website: www.elliedias.com
Facebook: Ellie Dias' Author Page
Email: ellie.dias@yahoo.com

To Janet Sadler
Treasured friend, confidante, mentor, collaborator,
and constant source of encouragement.

"I will not forget you.
I have written your name
On the palms of my hand."
~ Isaiah 49:15-16

INTRODUCTION

The Big Red Suitcase is missing in action, floating somewhere in cyberspace to parts unknown. Unsure when we will meet again, I'm halfway around the world in downtown Bangkok at midnight in the midst of a heated discussion with a strange man over what kind of underwear I should buy. As he dangles a pair of skimpy colored panties in my face, I think, "How the hell did I end up here after all those months spent planning my *trip of a lifetime*, my spiritual journey to the Himalayas?"

"You want to go *where*?"

"In this seed is the tree."

~ Dutch saying

As far back as I can recall, I've had a daring and inquisitive nature, always searching for new experiences to quench my over-the-top curiosity about the world around me. I'm a risk taker with an adventuresome spirit that has its roots in childhood.

Around the age of five, it was not unusual for me to travel far from the safety of my own yard to explore parts unknown, leaving my mother fraught with worry. Often, I would just head out in a new direction not knowing where I'd end up, solo, carefree, and happy. The older I got, the more I expanded my horizons, going into dark forests, finding and climbing into large drainage pipes, down abandoned shafts, and on a rare occasion a bat cave with a hollow passage under the earth—

anything that provided me with a challenge or something new and exciting.

I am also the type of person who, when passionate about something, gets quite headstrong and driven to experience it. Like the time I just had to fulfill a two-year desire to water ski nonstop around Butler's Island—a total of twenty-seven miles—on Lake Champlain in Vermont. At the age of fourteen, without my parents' knowledge and with an impending storm looming, I did just that, this time leaving them *both* sick with worry. Or when I decided one day that I *had* to learn how to play the piano. When I acquired this musical instrument free of charge, I neglected to tell my parents that I was bringing home a two-legged pea-green baby grand piano with the help of some friends. Unable to get the monstrosity into the house, or find a third leg, the unloved baby wound up hanging out on our front porch for six months until my dad got rid of it.

Those passions paled in comparison to the one I had about horses and my intense need to ride, which I satisfied at last when I took riding lessons at the age of fifty-three. Despite being kicked, peed on, falling in shit, almost decapitated and flung from horses galloping at breakneck speed, week after week I persevered until my body could no longer take the physical abuse.

It seems I was born to seek out unusual experiences that would fulfill my thirst for adventure. Little did I know they would set the stage for my thirty-year dream to travel to strange new lands.

Over the years, I had become so disillusioned with my Catholic upbringing that I found myself developing a strong attachment to Buddhist philosophy. As I cultivated a practice of daily meditation and intense contemplative thought, the more I wanted to experience it through culture. I longed to observe and partake of its rich spiritual beliefs and practices; to witness the compassionate nature of people who live according to the standard of simplicity that Buddha taught; to learn to detach myself from my Western roots and the pitfalls that come with self-indulgence and attachments to wealth, titles, and stuff. I longed to learn simplicity.

In the fall of 2007, I began to give some serious thought to going to Asia. The Greek language denotes two principles for time. *Chronos* is numeric, or chronological, time; and *Kairos*, the right or opportune moment, describes metaphysical, or divine, time. My *Chronos* and *Kairos* seemed aligned for this journey in the spring of 2009. By then I would be almost sixty-two. I found myself doing an extensive Internet search for Asian travel companies that drew me to Far Away Expeditions. I was enchanted reading about the three kingdoms of the Himalayas: Bhutan, Nepal, and Tibet—they were so rich in Buddhist culture and religion.

I contacted the travel agency to get more in-depth information about the trip and to discuss the price. The trip would cost me close to $8,000, and they required a deposit. I wrote the check, sealed the envelope, and sent it to them for safekeeping. Or so I assumed.

I spent the next several weeks trying to schedule a first-class round-trip ticket with my frequent-flyer miles. No easy feat but after days of persistence, I secured one. Things seemed to be falling into place until I discovered, quite by accident, that my flight plan was missing an important segment—JFK Airport in New York to Singapore via Frankfurt.

After an unpleasant conversation with the US Air agent, I was informed that the entire trip would have to be rebooked. Thirty minutes later the agent took me off hold and said, "Ellie, you're all set. I have rebooked you on the same flights, with the same dates, and first-class all the way." The agent's parting words, "Thank you for traveling with US Air, Ellie," would come back to haunt me in a matter of hours. Later that day while reviewing my emailed itinerary I saw that the agent had ticketed me with my nickname, which didn't match my passport. In disbelief, and more than a little pissed off, I called US Air again and was told I would have to rebook, *again*. They say, third time's a charm. I assumed I'd never hear that dreaded word *rebook* again. You know what they say about assumptions.

In the meantime, I still hadn't received anything from the travel agency—no trip information and no red t-shirt with their logo, both of which would be sent as soon as they received my deposit. I began calling and leaving messages. No call-backs. I emailed everyone and anyone at the travel agency. No response. This should have been a red flag, in fact a big red flag.

Trying to make some connection, I decided to Google their website. I was about to click on their link when my eyes glanced at the line below it stating that Far Away Expeditions was declaring bankruptcy. What was I going to do now? Was this it? Was this the end of my thirty-year dream? Was I ready to cut my losses, pack it in, and accept defeat? Not by a long shot. I was like a dog with a bone, but this dog was determined to get to the Himalayas.

Facing all these obstacles, frustrations, and doubts, one would think I should have had a change of heart. But I never wavered. I remained steadfast in keeping my dream alive at all costs. I'm not sure why. Perhaps it was my grit and determination that wouldn't allow me to give up despite the louder, more practical voice that kept trying to drown out my inner calling.

Enter Asian Pacific Adventures—my lifesaver. Within a few days, they put together an extensive day-by-day travel itinerary that included everything I hoped to see and more. I felt as if the universe was on my side at last. I soon learned the universe wasn't quite done with me yet.

On April 13, less than two weeks before my departure date, I read online: "Bangkok Civil Unrest: A State of Emergency Declared in Bangkok in Recent Days." Demonstrators were smashing doors and windows in hotels and racing through the buildings. And to top it off, a few links stated: "Reconsider your need to travel." I sat at the computer in disbelief. I was scheduled to fly to Bangkok for some touring before I headed to the Himalayas. And that was not the only declaration that put me in a holding pattern. A little thing called the swine flu had reached pandemic proportions. All across Asia, strict surveillance measures were in place and people were being quarantined. Sit tight, my travel agent said. A week before my departure I was given the green light. Although the flu was still rampant, the ban was lifted in Bangkok, and I thought, "Just get me on that damn plane before anything else happens!"

CHAPTER ONE

"It's way too heavy, Ellie!"

May 4, 2009, Home

It's an ominous sight. It's red, *incredibly red,* and huge. It's packed to the hilt and looks as if it's going to explode on contact. For the first time, I see it fully packed. It seems bigger and heavier the closer I get. It appears as if *I* could fit inside with ease, if it were empty, which it's not. It beckons me to pick it up. Knowing I must do this many times during the next three and a half weeks as I travel halfway around the world, I attempt to lift it. It doesn't budge. I try again, this time using the proper body mechanics that I learned in nursing school. All I manage to do is move it from side to side, where it topples over with a resounding thud. I stare at it. I struggle to get it upright. The friggin' thing is *heavy*. Suddenly an inner voice speaks to me. *It's way too heavy, Ellie. You'd better take some stuff out.* Meet the Big Red Suitcase, hereafter fondly referred to as *Big Red*.

I reach down to open the red monstrosity, unsure of what I can jettison. Before my hand even touches the zipper another voice asks me, *Ellie, how can you travel without all your must-haves, the safety items, color-coordinated outfits, rolls of toilet paper, bags of candy and trail mix, all so crucial for your trip of a lifetime?*

My husband, Ron, calls. "Come on Ellie, we'd better get started if you don't want to miss your flight." I groan as I wrestle it upright again and pull it out of the bedroom for its first meeting with Ron. Struggling to maneuver it through the hallway as it bangs into furniture and walls along the way, I think that of *all* the things I planned and prepared for, I should have at least once attempted to pick up this incredible hulk before taking off—alone—to parts unknown.

With all my strength, I drag Big Red over the threshold of our front door and to our Jeep, where Ron is waiting. I watch as he looks at me, at it, and back at me. He says, "Don't you think that's a little much to take?" I don't answer as I run back into the house. I come out with an overstuffed carry-on over one shoulder and clutching a briefcase with my laptop in it in the other hand. My body is off balance as I lean to the left. Incredulous, he asks, "More?"

Before I can respond, he stoops to pick up Big Red. Fortunately, he doesn't have to bend too far because it's as tall as it is big. It won't budge, even for him. He groans, "My back!" followed by "Jesus, Ellie, you need to take some stuff out."

Although this rings a bell—I know I read something about how much to bring in some travel literature—it seems like a ridiculous question to ask someone who has been planning, preparing, and organizing her *stuff* for months.

"I know it's a little hefty." I say.

"A *little?*" he replies.

"Yes, but I need everything in that suitcase; besides it'll all make me feel at home."

Ron looks at me. *"For the jungle?"* he asks.

For this, I have no answer. I offer to help. As we heave it into the hatch he says, "Really, Ellie, this thing is unmanageable."

With Big Red hunkered down in the back, we head to Boston's Logan Airport, where I will depart for JFK in New York, where my long-planned travels to the fabled Three Kingdoms of the Himalayas will begin.

We arrive at the airport and decide to check in curbside. I watch Ron struggle to hoist Big Red out. Once again his words flash through my brain. But I know beyond any reasonable doubt that I need absolutely everything in that suitcase to survive this adventure. It never dawns on me that my packing does not jibe with the fact that I am about to spend almost a month exploring a part of the world that warrants only t-shirts and jeans. Nor do I ever stop to think that I must pull, push, and somehow lift this mammoth beast, by myself, through twenty-two airports. Only when it is too late, will I realize the one thing I needed most—and should have packed before anything else—is common sense.

Ron rolls Big Red up to the check-in counter, hugs and kisses me good-bye, and wishes me smooth sailing—words destined to become the antithesis of my adventure. I enter the first airport terminal of my journey with great confidence, despite a nagging feeling about the weight and bulk of my luggage, unaware of how short-lived this feeling will be.

CHAPTER TWO

"Life is either a daring adventure or nothing."
~ Helen Keller

Off to the lands of simplicity and happiness!

So here's the itinerary: May 4 from Logan Airport in Boston to JFK Airport in New York, I will arrive in Bangkok the morning of May 6 and hit the ground running with a private tour of the Grand Palace where the Emerald Buddha temple resides. The next morning I head to Paro, the capital of Bhutan. It's a tiny Buddhist kingdom surrounded by the Himalayan Mountains and considered the last Shangri-La on the planet. I will be there for six days, during which I will visit the Tiger's Nest monastery 10,000 feet above sea level, hiking there through forests and up mountains dotted with fluttering prayer flags. I will journey over the La Dochu Pass and view the highest unclimbed peak in the world. I will meet Bhutanese people as I visit their markets and farmhouses, watch their favorite pastime, archery, and so much more.

On May 13, I will fly over Mt. Everest to Kathmandu, the capital of Nepal. I will view the most photographed Buddhist monument, Boudhanath (125 feet tall and 328 feet in circumference). I will experience a Nepalese village that is just as it was a hundred years ago, where I will meet some local people. After leaving Kathmandu, I'll head to a jungle resort in Nepal to take nature walks and view wildlife from atop an elephant. There will be Jeep drives, jungle treks, and bird watching during my three-day stay. Then I fly back to Kathmandu for more sightseeing of ancient palaces and temples.

Leaving Kathmandu again, I head to Lhasa. Once acclimated to the change in altitude I will visit the holiest site in Tibet, the Jokhang Temple. I will travel to different locations, visiting palaces, monasteries, and a Tibetan hospital. After several days, I return to Kathmandu and depart for Bangkok on May 26 to start my trip home.

To my family and friends: I promise not to arrive back on American soil garbed in a one-sleeved, maroon sarong with a shaved head or a dot on my forehead, but I might be whispering a chant. Having prepared for every facet of this journey, I have no doubt that my *trip of a lifetime* will be memorable in ways I can't even imagine. Wish me a safe and exciting adventure!

CHAPTER THREE

The battle of wills begins!

May 4, Oasis Lounge, JFK airport

There will be no picture of me in my May 4 blog post. I look like something the cat dragged in, and I haven't even left US soil. It all began the moment Ron left me with Big Red at the curb at Logan Airport in Boston.

The attendant at the check-in counter was a big guy who moaned when he lifted her onto the scale. "Miss, your suitcase weighs in at ninety-five pounds, way over the domestic weight limit. Would you like to remove something? If not, it will cost you one hundred dollars."

I did consider for a moment taking out the three cans of mosquito spray along with the half-gallon jug of Permethrin to protect me from dengue fever, or the ten bags of trail mix, power bars, crackers, and cheese. All these items amounted to about forty dollars give or take a few bucks.

I kept going back and forth in my mind. *Should I risk getting dengue fever or pay the hundred bucks?* No choice there. I wouldn't leave the Permethrin or the mosquito spray behind, nor would I get rid of any of my treats, unsure of how my taste buds would react to Asian food—especially those yak burgers. So I did what most sane people wouldn't; I paid the hundred-dollar excess baggage fee believing it was a small price to pay to stay true to my conviction that I needed absolutely everything in Big Red.

As I walked to the gate, I saw my flight was delayed. I was concerned about making my Singapore connection at JFK. When making my travel plans I worried endlessly about this and whether I should leave on an earlier flight, but the thought of hanging around JFK for nine hours didn't appeal to me.

For me, being stuck in an airport is as painful as a root canal. I had no idea that hanging around them would soon become my new reality.

I approached the desk and found I could still make the earlier flight to JFK. However, all I could think about was making sure Big Red would make the same flight. I couldn't imagine being without my clothes, traveling pharmacy, and survival gear. As the agent checked me in, she told me she would be able to retrieve my suitcase from my scheduled flight. When she asked me for a bag identifier, I only had to say big, bigger, biggest, and red.

After landing at JFK, I went straight to baggage claim and walked over to the luggage carousel. There she was, ready to greet me—Big Red! Smiling to myself and with a sigh of relief, I bent down to lift her off the belt. Picture this: I weigh one hundred pounds with no upper body strength and a bad shoulder. On the conveyor belt was my enormous suitcase weighing in at ninety-five pounds. You do the math. As I leaned in and grabbed the handle, I fell onto the moving carousel and proceeded to travel a short distance until I scrambled off with the help of an amused bystander. With something so heavy and no leverage, it was not an easy transition from the carousel to the floor, and after several unsuccessful attempts, I waited until the track stopped moving, clutched the handle, got her to the edge, and shoved her over. As I jumped back so she wouldn't land on my feet, people close to me followed suit. Once again Ron's words, *"Way too heavy, Ellie,"* came to mind. That phrase was becoming a mantra of sorts.

To save myself the five-buck rental for one of those luggage pushcarts, I carefully balanced my overstuffed carry-on and laptop on top of Big Red and began to pull her to the next terminal. I got no more than a few feet when Big Red began to tilt and fall over along with my laptop and carry-on. *"Way too heavy, Ellie,"* my mind chanted. What should have followed was *"Way too much stuff."* I was determined to make this work. I righted the suitcase, repositioned all my stuff, and took two steps followed by a repeat performance.

As travelers zoomed past me pushing their five-dollar carts with ease, I moved on to my next option and rented a cart. Once again I was faced with trying to lift Big Red. As I struggled, a kind soul came to my assistance. "You must be going away for a long time—your suitcase is pretty heavy." I half smiled. One would think I'd begin to see the light, or the load as it were, now that perfect strangers were echoing Ron's comments.

With all my stuff secured, I was ready to go, but no matter how hard I pushed that cart it wouldn't budge an inch. I walked back and reread the directions. I mean, how hard could this be? Irritated, I said out loud, "Of all the carts, I get the broken one." In frustration, I decided if I couldn't push it I would drag the freaking thing to the next terminal.

I towed the heavy cart along, getting only a few feet before everything fell off with a crash. I stared at the heap on the floor, completely fed up. I looked up and saw someone in an airport uniform watching me. I called out to him, telling him I had a faulty cart and wanted my money back and a new cart. He yelled out: "Lady, maybe if you push the handle bar down, it will release the brake." I almost yelled back, "Are you kidding me?"

Pushing Big Red with all my might, I found Singapore Airline's first-class check-in line. Waiting my turn, I thought, *"I've been through enough; what more could possibly go wrong?"* Fateful words.

As I stepped forward, I tried to lift Big Red and couldn't.

The agent was kind enough to get off her seat to help me. She strained as she attempted to lift it and asked if there was a dead body in there. As she put the suitcase on the scale, she announced, "Your bag is too heavy; do you have another bag to lighten it up?" I could hear Ron's voice again with that phrase again: *"Way too heavy, Ellie."* I asked if I could pay for the extra weight as I had in Boston, but she informed me it was an unacceptable weight even for first-class. Thankfully my friend Pat had given me a duffel bag for any souvenirs. It was inside the suitcase. I told the agent I had to find it. She said no problem; she would wait to process me.

So, there I was, first in line but down on all fours on the airport floor, with people behind and on both sides of me as I opened this perfectly packed suitcase to locate the duffel bag. Of course, it was on the bottom, and no matter how hard I tried to dig it out, the only way I could get to it was to take *everything* out. I pulled out my neatly ironed tops and capris, moving on to my shoes while being careful not to bring my personals into view. When one of my numerous rolls of toilet paper escaped and rolled across the floor toward a passenger in a different line, the agent asked me to move out of the way. Not only was I holding up traffic, I was blocking it with Big Red, and all my stuff.

On my hands and knees, I dragged Big Red to a corner they designated just for me. Still unable to locate the duffel bag, I was in a panic. I started tossing out underwear, shoes, socks, and bags of trail mix onto the floor. A can of my mosquito repellent, accompanied by yet another roll of toilet paper, headed in the direction of the next line of passengers. I was now almost lying flat on the floor with one arm outstretched, trying to retrieve them. Someone nonchalantly kicked my things back over to me: woman on the airport floor, head in a suitcase, ass in the air, with stuff flying everywhere. At least Big Red kept me hidden.

I finally found the duffel bag and began to jam whatever

I could inside it. Into the random mess went various bras, shoes, dresses, toilet paper rolls, and trail mix bags. Outside the suitcase and lying on its side was my half-gallon jug of Permethrin spray tangled up in an article of clothing. I paused for a moment realizing it was the second time that spray with its extra weight had attracted my attention. I almost tossed it out. But I was more driven by the memory of how much time and energy had gone into purchasing the one and only thing that could protect me from dengue fever. Back into the suitcase it went. So much for all the hours I'd spent packing with great care. A blind person couldn't have made a worse mess. I checked both bags, glad to be rid of them. In hindsight, I would eat my words.

Opening the door to the Singapore Airlines' first-class lounge, I realize I should have unloaded some of my precious belongings into that duffel bag back at Logan and saved one hundred dollars, not to mention the embarrassment of the repacking fiasco. Hopefully, this will be the last tortuous moment on my *trip of a lifetime.*

Flash forward: After my return home I will reread the documents from Asian Pacific Adventures. Under the heading BAGGAGE, it reads: "We suggest that you travel as light as possible, especially on trips to remote areas where there are no porters and you must carry everything yourself. Overweight baggage will be liable for excess baggage charges." In all my planning, how did I miss that? Truth be told, I'm sure I read it but was too hell-bent on taking everything I felt I needed to pay it any heed.

As I wait for my 9:15 P.M. departure to Frankfurt, my excitement wanes. Despite my years of practice, I have a nagging feeling of failure about how attached I am to material things, and how fearful I am to leave my *stuff* behind, even on a trip to the land of nonattachment. I begin repeating one of the calming mantras I have committed to memory and call on all my powers of relaxation. I start to relax and immediately shift my thoughts to all the rare and unusual opportunities ahead that will allow me to do more than talk the talk.

Finally settled into my first-class seat, I'm airborne with drink in hand. I think about all the challenges and obstacles I had to overcome to get this far. With newfound enthusiasm, I raise my glass and salute myself for making my thirty-year dream into reality.

CHAPTER FOUR

"It is the single step that begins the journey of
a thousand miles."

~ Tao Te Ching

Please, oh please, you gotta let me on!

I f only I had taken that single step in the right direction. When I took driving lessons at the age of sixteen, the instructor told my mom it might be impossible for me to pass the test because whenever he gave me instructions to turn left or stop, I always got it wrong. In his words, "It's like she's in a fog." Forty-six years later, I'm still in that fog.

May 5, Frankfurt, Germany

My departure experiences were frustrating and embarrassing. But when I raised my glass en route to Frankfurt, I assumed those mishaps were all behind me and began to find them humorous. It seems my levity was way too premature. Today, tonight, whatever time of day it is, embarrassment, anger, and everything in between don't even come close to describing my state of mind when I *missed* my flight to Singapore.

So how did this happen? Well, on arrival in Germany I faced a forty-five-minute layover before departing for Singapore. Since it was rather short, I decided not to stray far from the gate. I plunked my tired body onto a chair not five feet away from the gate. To be on the safe side, I frequently looked at the boarding sign. From an angle, I did see a green light flashing, but I never saw the words NOW BOARDING, which would have been my cue to get back on the plane.

When the forty-five-minutes had come and gone, I approach the gate and ask the agent when we would start boarding.

Surprised, she said, "Everyone has already boarded." I backed away in a panic and head toward the boarding ramp. The woman called out after me, "I am sorry, but it's too late to board now."

I stopped short, turned, and with my heart pounding in my chest ask: "You mean the plane has left?"

"No," she replied.

Breathing a sigh of relief, "Oh thank God, then just let me on."

She puts another nail in my coffin with "I can't do that. It's a security regulation; once the door is closed it can't be reopened."

My panic rose, I could see the door of the plane a stone's throw away. I plead, "Please let me on; I have to be on that plane or I will miss my connections!" To my horror, the answer was still no!

Stunned, I put my head on the counter and moaned. "This isn't happening. How could this be happening?" The gate agent tells me they'd not only announced the departure several times but had paged me three times, and I never showed up. Embarrassed, I look around to see if anyone can see how pathetic I'm acting. I spot a toddler screaming at her mother. I try to block out her cries and think, *I wish I could scream at someone, anyone.* I catch myself and silently begin to repeat over and over, "I am letting go, I am okay with this, I am letting go." A thought comes to me. *What would a Tibetan monk do in these circumstances? Probably pray and chant.* I think about it but realize my brand-new powder-blue outfit is not the look of a chanter, at least not in the middle of a crowded airport. Praying is safer. I pray.

"Sweet Jesus, help me out." Guess there are still some remnants of that Catholic girl lurking inside me.

Playing the scene over and over in my head, I remember hearing my name being called at least once. I rationalize that I didn't respond because I thought it wasn't me they were calling. I don't know anyone in Germany, so who would be paging me? And I have the gall to call myself an experienced flyer. Anger at myself surpasses all other emotions.

The gate agents quickly began to re-ticket me and get me back on track. As they attempt to locate flights for me, I berate myself again and again for missing this critical flight, bemoaning all the effort I'd put into securing first-class seating, menu planning, and the like. What a waste.

They find me a seat in first-class, but it means a ten-hour layover in Germany and creates a domino effect. I wouldn't arrive in Bangkok until 10 P.M. instead of 10 A.M., obliterating my private tour of the Grand Palace, one of the most spectacular examples of an ancient Siamese court, and the palace that houses the Emerald Buddha Temple. I was booked to stay in the heart of Bangkok at the luxurious Orchid Sheraton Hotel and Tower overlooking the river. Upon my return from sightseeing I was scheduled for a much-needed spa treatment and a relaxing evening before my 3:30 A.M. flight to Paro, Bhutan. All of this was scratched in the blink of an eye.

"Paging Eleanor Dias. Paging Eleanor Dias. Are you here? Are you here?" Yeah, I'm here all right—for a g-d damn ten hour wait.

With an endless stretch of time ahead of me, I look over my travel guide with all the exciting Bangkok adventures that would forever remain on the printed page. I will reach Bangkok just in time to flop into bed in my five-star hotel. I must be up at 1 A.M. to catch my four-hour flight to Bhutan, where they may get to greet a visitor who no longer cares about landing in the happiest place on Earth. Stay tuned. It can't get any worse. Can it?

In the meantime, if anyone is curious, Big Red departed on time to Bangkok. They assured me it would arrive ahead of me. What do you think the odds are of that happening? Any bets? I keep thinking about all those outfits I had packed for each day of my *trip of a lifetime*. Now it looks as if I will be in the same clothes and underwear for at least two days and counting. My idea of a perfectly planned trip didn't include a missed flight or the need to find underwear on-the-go. Otherwise, I would have heeded my travel agent's advice about having a well-stocked day pack including a change of underwear—which of course I don't have.

One thing I do have is my brand-new jaunty straw hat with the black ribbon. I was afraid to pack it in Big Red for fear it would get squashed. It hasn't been on my head yet but is still dutifully tied with a piece of yarn to my useless carry-on bag, and it looks perfect. William Makepeace Thackeray's quote comes to mind: "Good humor is one of the best articles of dress one can wear in society." I plop my straw hat on my head and try to smile as I enter the first-class lounge.

May 5, still trying to experience enlightenment in Frankfurt, Germany

I have now decided to add Where the hell is Ellie Dias? to the famous questions Where's Waldo? and Where in the world is Carmen Sandiego? I bet you're all wondering when this infamous *trip of a lifetime* is going to begin. So am I. It's going to be ten long, grueling hours here in Germany despite the first class lounge. I think that if I had to do this stint in the airport terminal, I'd kill myself or some unsuspecting soul. Talking to my husband, he offers this advice: "Just pack it in, Ellie. Cut your losses and come home."

Doubts begin to creep into my mind, *What am I doing here? Why did I come? What is the point of it, of any of it?* I shake off the uncertainty and second-guessing as I round another corner of the lounge. Taking a deep breath, I chant to myself, "It's okay. I'm fine. This will pass."

Six hours in, I try to occupy myself with something other than being pissed off. When I'm not beating myself up, I'm feeling sorry for myself. For the first time, I realize how much less stressful it would have been to have someone else along, not only to help navigate me, but Big Red as well. The truth was that no one was daring enough to accompany me, which I take as proof that I am destined to make this journey alone. I'm positive it's the only way I can immerse myself, without any distractions, in the nonmaterialistic lifestyle of the Himalayan people. Little do I know how *immersed* I will become.

After exploring the nooks and crannies of the lounge, I discover four beds tucked away in a dark, secluded room at the end of a hallway. Three are occupied. The empty one beckons. I settle in and pull up the blanket, hoping to sleep away my frayed nerves. Just as I start to doze, the guy next to me begins to entertain me with the serenade from hell. It's the kind that leaves your nerve endings feeling raw. Totally beyond the definition of irritating, it is the dreaded *snore*. His is not the soft, easy tone of someone sleeping in bliss, but one that rumbles like a freight train. To say that I'm feeling on edge doesn't even come close. Here I am, almost halfway around the world, and that sound is the *worst* noise in the universe. It requires you to stuff your ears with so many earplugs you feel as if you're going to swallow them. It's the sound that calls for an extra bedroom, has come between great relationships, and brings out my demonic personality; and the jerk is less than three feet away. Sitting up, I begin to make the full range of vocal sounds known to man. He doesn't miss a beat. I should have known better. I've had thirty-five years of experience with this kind of noise.

In case my readers are curious, snoring can reach sound levels up to seventy decibels and can cause certain health risks—like murder. Once that sound reaches eighty-five decibels, it can have adverse hearing effects on the listener. Deafness would be welcome. Frustrated to no end, and fed up with everything and everybody at this point, I want to go over and slap this guy silly. Not a practical solution. I lie back down, breathe deeply, and practice the Buddhist philosophy of loving-kindness for all beings. I swear, the more I try, the louder he gets. Screw the loving-kindness! I get up and walk over to his bed. I look down at that face, and it's all I can to do to keep from shoving my fingers up his nostrils and ripping his nose off. Instead, I kick his bed so hard it rocks. I quickly exit the premises. His response? You guessed it—he just snores louder.

I pace the perimeter for the umpteenth time, passing the huge floor-to-ceiling windows, where I watch plane after plane take off, whisking happy travelers to their destinations. The final four hours pass slowly as I wait my turn to join them. I feel and look a mess. What I wouldn't give for a hot shower and clean underwear. I'm so tired I actually think about packing it in as Ron suggested, but I am not a quitter. I refuse to accept defeat and stubbornly hang on to the thought that nothing else can go wrong. I think about what Buddha would do in my place. Simple answer. I practice deep breathing and meditation, silently repeating to myself, "All is well, all is well."

CHAPTER FIVE

Did you really say rebook?

May 5, in flight to Bangkok

Apparently, *nothing more can go wrong* isn't in the cards. After ten long hours with nothing to do but try to meditate, rest, and keep from grinding my teeth in frustration, I walk to the departure gate. My excitement returns: I'm realizing my dream. I'm on my way to Bangkok at last!

At the gate, I hand my ticket to the same agent from the day before. Mind you, I just assumed everything was in order, so I never bothered to look at it. It's not as if I didn't have a lot of time to check it out. I watch as she types in the necessary information, I see a frown on her face that makes my stomach churn. Before I could mouth the words "Now what?" she says, "There was a mistake made during your ticketing. We will have to void the whole thing and try to rebook you."

Of course, she has no idea how many times I've already been through this or how much I loathe the word, *rebook*. I don't know whether to laugh, cry, or throw up. But praise the Lord, with just moments to spare, she succeeds in getting me on the flight before the door to the jetway is closed and locked. She handed me my boarding card, but before I turn to go, I ask one important question. Had Big Red arrived as promised ten hours ago?

Remember that great line from *Apollo Thirteen*—"Houston,

we have a problem?" I'm adding it to my growing list of non-Buddhist-type chants. My new chant will be *Ellie, you have a problem.* The agent cheerily tells me my luggage is en route, but she doesn't know when it will arrive in Bangkok. With a reassuring voice, she just needs to know where I will be staying in Bangkok so my bags could be delivered. Well, guess what? After missing my flight, I'd emailed the travel agency to see if they could book me into a hotel closer to the airport. There was no point in spending all that money on an expensive hotel when I'd barely have time to see the bed. I hadn't heard back from them yet, so I had no idea where I'd end up. Will this nightmare ever end?

My seat on the Bangkok flight turns into a bed, and before my head hits the pillow, I grab my little bottle of Xanax. I down one with a glass of wine and refuse anything else. The saying *View each challenge from the highest perspective,* flutters to mind, followed by a resounding *Bullshit!* My *high* will be swallowing an extra Xanax for good measure. Certainly not the interpretation the author intended, I'm sure.

I lie back, relishing the silence and peace. I float into a relaxed state of bliss, relieved to be finally on my way.

CHAPTER SIX

My relationship with Catholicism
opens the door to Buddhism.

I was brought up in a traditional, middle-class household with a mother, father, and older brother. Our lifestyle was anything but uneventful; in truth it was chaotic. Our home was where displaced relatives and their baggage, most of which didn't show up in any suitcase—red or not—came to stay for periods ranging from a few days to a few months. In addition, my father's hot-and-cold temper made for disruptive living conditions. He could be loving one minute, then fly into a rage over the most inconsequential thing. His explosive anger, which often included threats of physical abuse, were directed at my mother and brother, never at me. For whatever the reason I was not in his line of fire. Because he treated me like the *perfect child who could do no wrong*, I learned at an early age that being perfect was my ticket to being loved. He mellowed over the years, resulting in more peaceful family relationships.

Our strict Catholic upbringing was enforced by my mother. Her faith was so strong that my father converted from Judaism when he married her. Church attendance and catechism classes were mandates, and unlike my brother, I wanted this discipline and code. From childhood into my early twenties, church was a place I felt protected, a place that offered the sense of peace I longed for—or so I believed.

In my teens I was completely tethered to my religious traditions and beliefs. My relationship with God was intense. I believed the only way I could attain His everlasting love was to be a model of perfection—a sure setup for failure, because I always felt in need of being *fixed*. My daily mission was to make sure I was free from sin in every thought and action. It was next to impossible to live up to those Catholic girl standards, and that left me in a constant whirlwind of self-criticism. I feared I might never get it right. It was a long and painful journey before I turned my back on the church, releasing its choke hold on me.

I had attended Mass faithfully, made endless novenas, and diligently practiced keeping the Commandments. When I faltered, I went to confession so I would be in a pure state at Mass on Sunday morning.

The guilt accumulated over the years and became my personal cross to bear. In the end confession served only one purpose: to fill me with negative self-talk and bad feelings that were way out of proportion to any sins I had committed. Sometimes I think about how different my perspective would have been had I known the Buddhist philosophy on the subject of guilt. "Remembering a wrong is like carrying a burden on the mind," said Buddha. All those years of living with a reward-and-punishment system laid the foundation for the seeds of Buddhism to germinate within me when the time was right.

CHAPTER SEVEN

A baby elephant, polite underwear, and a Thai t-shirt all in one night!

When people plan trips, their course is usually more or less on target. Not mine. Despite being a manic perfectionist, and one of the best planners in the world, my travel adventure—my thirty-year dream—was more than a journey. A *trip* in the broadest sense of the word, it plays out like a crazy drama.

If someone had told me months earlier that I would be buying underwear at midnight, on the other side of the world, with a strange man who barely speaks English, I would have laughed in their face.

May 6, Orchid Sheraton Hotel and Tower, Bangkok

It's time for the next round of "Ellie's Not So Excellent Adventure." I've stopped calling it the *trip of a lifetime*.

I arrive in Bangkok around 11 P.M. Thankfully, I'm alert enough to see the sign with my name on it as soon as I get off the plane. A lovely young girl named Apple (yep, even in Bangkok) helps me through immigration. Since I'm not coughing or sneezing, I easily pass the swine flu check-point. I must tell you that the swine flu was an unwelcome addition to my trip. In every terminal, giant maps highlight the locations of current swine flu outbreaks—essentially everywhere I'm headed. Screeching to a halt whenever someone near me coughs or sneezes, I'm too paranoid to blow my nose in public for fear I might be detained indefinitely.

Good news: Apple informs me that Big Red, has been found. Bad news: it was still somewhere in Germany. Good news: it will arrive in Bhutan, followed by the bad news that it will not get there until the eighth, maybe. Sarcastically I ask if it is coming by yak.

They give me one hundred dollars in Bangkok money for essentials, and I can only think of one thing. Underwear. It is almost midnight, so nothing in the airport is open. There's a distinct possibility that I will be wearing these clothes for at least two more days—a reminder of the wasted fashionable and clean clothing still stuffed inside Big Red.

Apple introduces me to my guide, and informs him of my luggage predicament. I shake his hand and blurt out, "I need *underwear!*" I couldn't care less about being shy, polite, or politically correct. He shrugs, smiles, and off we go. They sure are good-natured here. Just imagine what the response would be if you said that to a strange man in the US.

Sitting in the back of the van, I can hear my guide and the driver in deep discussion about where they can take me to get underwear at midnight. As we drive around the outskirts of the city, I think again about that "well-stocked day pack," which I do not have. I'm reminded once more of what I do have in my carry-on bag: a plethora of makeup and jewelry, plus just about everything else I don't need. Ahh, my Western mind-set rears its ugly ahead again—too *much* stuff and never the *right* stuff.

Nothing is open at this hour, so we head to downtown Bangkok and the Pat Pong night market. The driver drops us off in front of a dark alley that leads to a rather chaotic marketplace. I swear Bangkok's entire population of ten million is here. It's body-to-body crowds shopping, eating at sidewalk vendors, rowdy partying, and over-the-top craziness from the nearby go-go bars. What an assault on the senses. I'm exhausted, and the last place I want to be is this hot, sweaty, noisy place.

I'm known for my need for peace and quiet. I abhor loud noises, especially unexpected ones. I never have the radio or TV on in my home. Even in my car, the radio is off. For a moment, I wish I was back on the plane, nestled under a warm blanket, soothed by wine and Xanax: but this is no time for wishing. I am on a mission to find underwear so I can begin my journey to the three kingdoms of the Himalayas. I want to leave the deafening noise behind and replace it with the silence of Buddhist temples. Little do I know I'm in for a big surprise.

Keep in mind that my guide is the person who was supposed to show me the Grand Palace. Instead, he is weaving me in and out of little market stands looking for underwear. Not long into our shopping excursion, I find some. I grab the first size small I see. Small, clean, and white will do it for me. However, my guide doesn't approve of my selection. He picks a pair of skimpy, colored panties and dangles them in my face. This is a little too personal for comfort. I don't want to hurt his feelings, so I let him select a t-shirt for me to sleep in. I am now the proud owner of a four-dollar Thai national flag t-shirt and three pairs of panties with S.POLITE.COM on the waistband. My first Asian souvenirs!

I still need some toiletries, so we head to a twenty-four-hour supermarket. Wandering the aisles—not one label is in English—I am at the mercy of my guide to pick out what I need. I must admit he does a lot better this time. He hands me a raspberry-smelling deodorant stick, some flavored toothpaste, a pink toothbrush, and pink socks. With each item he chooses he gives me a wide, toothless grin. My travel agent was right—you would be hard pressed to find a dentist around here. My guide wants to continue shopping for me, but I have all the *essentials* I need for the time being. What more could I want? Well, Big Red would be nice.

So much for the outfits I had packed for each day, along with enough shoes to outfit a family. Again I wonder, w*ho does this, Ellie?* adding Ron's, *"Do you really need all that stuff?"* to my growing mantra list. Is this some underlying message I'm supposed to be getting?

As we walk back to the car, we see a panhandler with a baby elephant on a leash in the midst of all the noise and craziness. This image will forever remind me of all the great sights I have missed: the Grand Palace with its incredible architecture and intricate detail; the highly revered Buddha meticulously carved from a single block of emerald; the floating markets where hundreds of wooden boats crowd the river, each one filled to the brim with farm-fresh fruits, vegetables, and flowers. Oh, how I want to see all this and more. Such a disappointment, all because I didn't hear the page "Will Eleanor Dias please come to the departure gate. We are now boarding." Not just once, but three times.

We finally get to my hotel at 1 in the morning. After taking a quick shower, I post to my blog. I decide it isn't worth going to sleep since I'm leaving in an hour for my four-hour flight to Paro, where "happiness is everywhere." Oh, to be happy again! I pause, gazing out the window at the crystal-clear night and the Chao Phraya River. Called the River of Kings, it is considered the lifeblood of Bangkok. I love how its calm waters reflect the sparkling lights of the temples and glistening skyscrapers. Here I sit in my Thai national t-shirt, musing over the unforeseen events of the last few days. I find it ironic how the barest essentials are getting me through my first days and nights of this adventure after my meticulous plans went so awry. So much for the time and effort I put into packing Red in an attempt to create a perfect *trip of a lifetime*. I should have spent less time meditating and reading about Buddhism and had some therapy before I left home. Better yet, I should have attended Over-Packers Anonymous.

CHAPTER EIGHT

"Be Prepared"

~ Boy Scout motto

When I received the three separate ten-page documents about what to expect and what to bring on my adventure in Bhutan, Nepal, and Tibet, I had my work cut out for me. I approached this trip with a level of preparation appropriate for taking the bar exam. After reading countless guidebooks cover-to-cover, I made long to-do lists, reviewing and revising them many times over. I was confident my *trip of a lifetime* would be smooth sailing from start to finish. Or so I thought.

Being a wardrobe fanatic, my focus was on clothing. I had twenty-two days to pack for, and I attempted to have a different outfit for each day. I wanted to look picture-perfect at all times. This is how I tend to navigate through life. *Every day* of a sixteen-week semester as a college professor, I wore a different outfit, complete with matching jewelry and shoes.

I went on a shopping spree. Where most people would simply pack jeans and t-shirts, I bought an array of capri pants with matching tops, colorful scarves, and sundresses with coordinating hats, along with five pairs of the cutest sandals and two pairs of fashionable sneakers. When I took a moment to remind myself that I would be spending almost three days in the Nepali jungle, I did throw in a pair of jeans, fashionable jeans. Although I read it, I paid no attention to the *what to bring* section of the travel agent's documents, which emphasized the following: Do not bring delicate clothes. Comfortable, practical clothes are essential. Footwear should be durable, supportive, and comfortable. The most important sentence of all, *the lighter you pack, the better*, would come back to bite me in the ass, again and again.

Keeping in mind the climate changes between the three kingdoms, I had to be ready for a range of weather from warm, to cool, to cold. So onto the growing pile went a winter hat, a turtleneck, a pair of gloves, and long johns. It did cross my mind, albeit briefly, that these last few articles of clothing were better suited for someone hiking up to the Mt. Everest base camp. Not that I was going anywhere near there, but my thought was *it could get really cold, so best be prepared*. It still didn't register that the parts of Asia I would be traveling to were not known for resort wear. By concentrating on my wardrobe, I somehow missed the essence of the minimalist nature of Buddhism. In hindsight, I became an oxymoron of sorts—some would say leave the *oxy* out. I was intent on packing and carting all my *stuff* while forgetting the purpose of my journey: to free myself from my Western *attached* way of being. I neglected to practice what the Buddha meant about clinging and attachment as an impediment to spiritual freedom. If I had, I might have packed a hell of a lot lighter. Instead, my stuff weighed me down, becoming just another ball and chain to contend with. Only this time halfway around the world.

My shopping list for the nonclothing items was also extensive. I packed a first-aid kit, antiseptic creams, insect repellent, and enough toilet paper for all occasions. On the list was a highlighted recommendation to have a well-stocked day pack should you ever become separated from your luggage. Critical advice for me *if only I had heeded it*.

Also, on *my* packing list were medications and nutritional supplements. I take eighteen different supplements on a daily basis plus several prescription drugs. Together that came to a staggering 484 pills for a twenty-two-day trip. The tricky part was finding a way to fit them into a suitcase already on the verge of exploding. Looking back, I wonder who in their right mind takes that many pills, let alone takes them on a trip halfway around the world? Did I really believe I couldn't live without supplements such as turmeric, garlic, and CoQ10 for twenty-two days? Wouldn't a multivitamin suffice? I took every last one of them along, plus medications for motion and altitude sicknesses. I had a daily routine, and I would stick to it no matter where I was going, even to the soaring Himalayas and mighty Nepali jungle.

Then there were my snacks. I brought bags, and more bags, of trail mix, dried fruit, energy bars, peanut butter crackers, cheese crackers, and all sorts of packaged candy—plenty of nourishment for when I was crisscrossing the countryside. I added a little extra to my stash just in case my palette didn't agree with the food on the menu. Yet my adventurous spirit meant I was game to try anything and everything available. I would truly eat those words.

I packed all the usual items such as deodorant and toothpaste and then added a new loofa to accompany my favorite shower gel and lotion, a small bottle of Woolite to hand wash my delicates, and a Waterpik. Never can tell when you might need a Waterpik in the jungle.

At Walmart, I purchased plastic boxes with inserts for my pharmacy, and adaptors for all my electrical equipment, which included my laptop, white-noise machine, hair dryer, curling iron, and two cameras. In the same aisle, I saw luggage compression bags. I read on the back of the package that by placing my clothes in the plastic bags and forcing out the air, my clothes would take up less space. I grabbed three different sizes. Now I could bring more clothes.

In between all my prepping, packing, and procuring the appropriate visas, I got a dental checkup, because "dentists are hard to find." I discovered you only had to look at the locals to know that this was true. Then I focused my attention on getting immunized against such diseases as hepatitis A and B, polio, and typhus.

Apprehensive about everything I needed to remember while traveling, I started making notes on index cards, which I highlighted and laminated so I could use them as study guides. By the time I was ready to depart I had enough cards to fill a small suitcase on their own.

Asian Pacific Adventures suggested I read as much as possible about the countries and their cultures and learn some key phrases before I left. My valiant attempts fell flat as I tried to pronounce simple things like *kadinche* (thank you), *kuzo zangpo la* (hello), and *ga de bay Ye* (how are you?) One phrase I really should have given more effort to was *chopsa gateh mo*? (where is the toilet?)

My list included getting camera ready. I had a new, sophisticated, digital camera and a small memory camcorder, each accompanied by a booklet full of confusing instructions and way too many options. Learning all these possibilities to the nth degree became a major undertaking that only someone like me would attempt. This led to a need to create still more index cards to ensure I wouldn't forget anything. By the time I was ready to leave, I would have given my firstborn just to be able to aim and shoot with a disposable camera.

When it came time to pack Big Red, I tried what I thought was a logical approach. I spent hours methodically folding and stacking my clothes to coincide with the order of each country I would visit, a practice in futility. Then I made a valiant attempt to use those compression bags. I struggled to get my clothes into them. I sat on them and rolled, trying to squeeze and squash out the air. Giving up, I packed my stuff the old-fashioned way, finishing with the classic comic move: I sat on the suitcase so I could zip it shut. It bulged like a pregnant elephant. It was filled with everything but the kitchen sink—*stuff* that no one bound for the farms and jungles of the Himalayas will ever need. Suitcase ready? Check.

And finally, because I wanted to share my big adventure with family and friends, my daughter created the blog Trip of a Lifetime. I was confident they would soon be thinking, "Oh, how we wish we were there."

CHAPTER NINE

Bhutan—Mystical Land of the Thunder Dragon

"Boo-tan, Boo-tawn? What? Where is that?" It seems everyone was clueless about this tiny, landlocked kingdom of 700,000. I'd never heard of it until I decided to go there and began to research this mysterious place. Located in the eastern Himalayas, it is squeezed between the two most populated nations in the world, India and China.

For more than a thousand years it has been known as Druk Yul, Land of the Thunder Dragon, and the divine madman.

Many consider it to be the last Shangri-La, and possibly the happiest place on Earth. Until the 1960s, its landscape cut it off from the outside world. With no roads, no cars, no telephones or electricity—it only recently got television. Until 1974, the country maintained a self-imposed isolation with no tourists allowed. Since then, the country has limited the number of visitors to about 25,000 a year.

As I read about Bhutan before my trip—the mesmerizing landscape, ancient temples clinging to magnificent mountaintops, dense forests, warm and inviting people—I developed a longing to see what those who'd traveled there had experienced. What sealed the deal for me was when I read that in 1972, former King Jigme Singye Wangchuck had coined the term Gross National Happiness. In 2009, the *New York Times* quoted the Bhutan's prime minister as saying that "greed, insatiable human greed" is what he sees in the world. He went on to state that the goal of gross national happiness is not happiness itself, but a state of being that each person must define for himself. The aim is to define the quality of life in holistic and psychological terms rather than materialistic ones. This philosophy is the country's blueprint for survival as it transitions toward democracy and modernization. It would be the perfect start both to my *trip of a lifetime* and my quest to create a lifestyle more aligned with the values of the East.

Included in the packet was information about customs. They have a great respect for their culture and expect the same respect from visitors. They speak English, and when talking often place their right hand in front their mouths to avoid defiling the air. One article explained that it's considered rude to question or pursue certain issues with them. It's also best to accept the reasons given, such as it is inconvenient to visit certain places or take pictures in certain temples. The Bhutanese find it impolite to say no, unlike the Western world. Could anyone in the US survive a day, an hour, or even a minute with these cultural dictates?

It's considered bad manners to appear too sure of oneself or too firm in one's opinion. Those of us in the West would rather die than abide by this social custom. We do have one thing in common: receiving a guest without offering them something to drink is the height of rudeness.

Several people who had recently returned from Bhutan encouraged me to experience this tiny kingdom while its rich culture is still intact. I couldn't resist the urge to see the fabled land of the thunder dragon, a country of Buddhists, yaks, alpine valleys, and snow-capped peaks. Seventy percent of the people who live in the happiest place on Earth are farmers living in small rural hamlets accessible only on foot. I wanted to observe a culture that is among the oldest, most carefully guarded, and best preserved in the world. A place where cigarettes are banned, new buildings or private homes are constructed using traditional techniques, and a dress code was established by the government in 1980 that made it compulsory for citizens to wear the country's national dress when in public. Captivated, mesmerized, and enchanted by all that I read, I just had to see this mystical kingdom.

May 7, On the way to Paro, Bhutan

With my perky straw hat perched on my head, I'm still traveling light, dressed in my *no longer new* powder-blue outfit accented by an ink stain from a pen rupture. I'm sure glad I packed that bottle of Woolite. Big Red is still who-knows-where atop a yak, and although I am missing my belongings, I relish the fact that I didn't have to do battle with her going through the last two airport terminals and baggage claim carousels.

I'm sitting next to a former Buddhist monk while we wait for the flight to board. He had left the order, gotten married, and has a thirteen-year-old daughter who lives with him in Bhutan. He intends to return to the order in a few years because his wife wants to stay in India. No religious penalty here, just another reason I'm enamored with Buddhism.

I have a bird's-eye view of the capital as we come out of the clouds. The peaks of the Himalayas that surround Paro are breathtaking. The rice paddies and farmhouses sit nestled against the mountains. A red-and-white temple comes into sight, and prayer flags are blowing everywhere. I can't wait to land.

"Is this your first time flying into Paro?" the gentleman next to me asks. I nod, and he begins to tell me what to expect from the descent—something I hadn't read about. Classified as *the* most dangerous and terrifying landing in the world we will be flying between some of the world's tallest peaks. To add to the excitement, the runway is carved out of the mountain foliage, making it difficult to see until the plane is at 500 feet. Pilots must fly through the vicious winds that sweep across the valley. *Great*, I think. I've always felt that turbulence is a fate worse than death. I can take anything except a rough ride. He feels compelled to inform me that there are only eight—that's right, *eight*—pilots certified to land at this airport. Almost as an afterthought, he adds that the lack of flat land will make it appear as if we are going in at an angle more appropriate for a crash landing. Certainly not for the faint of heart.

His final words before our descent were, "Hang on to your hat. It's going to be quite a ride. You might want to close your eyes."

Never one to listen to advice, I look out the window and see dozens of houses sprinkled across the mountain range. The plane takes several sharp-angled turns, coming within what appears to be a few feet of clipping their roofs. As my seatmate had predicted, strong winds seem to come out of nowhere, causing severe turbulence. I tighten my seat belt. There is no time to panic or practice deep breathing because gut-wrenching motion sickness has already kicked in. As I lean forward, reaching for the barf bag, I think, *Fifteen years of air travel and I've never had to use one of these until now.* I want to die as I break my record and hurl!

My rather smelly powder-blue outfit is now sporting ink *and* puke stains—hardly the image I'd planned.

A little unsteady, and more than slightly disheveled, I was profoundly grateful when the plane finally touched down. I step onto the tarmac facing a huge sign: 100 YEARS OF PEACE, UNITY & HAPPINESS.

My heart swells as I whisper, "I'm finally here." I manage to find my way to immigration, where my visa is waiting for me just as planned. Entering the baggage claim area with nothing to claim, I immediately spot my name held up by my guide, Yeshey. Both he and my driver, Dawa, wear robes called *gho*—the traditional dress for men. These floor-length robes are hiked up to the knees and tied at the waist with a hand-woven belt and are accompanied by long socks. Wondering what the female version looks like, I desperately think I might have to buy one if I can't get this smell out of my clothes. Who knows when I will be reunited with Big Red and my wardrobe? However, the thought of another shopping spree with a strange man is not how I want to begin my Bhutan adventure.

Yeshey already knows about my luggage situation, relieving me of trying to explain why I look and smell so bad. Our first stop is the Silver Pine Hotel, where I am warmly greeted by a gho-clad young boy and a girl dressed in a *kira,* the traditional female attire. The kira is draped across the body over a blouse and fastened at the shoulders with silver clasps. A *toego,* or jacket,

is worn over it. Rather cute and quite fashionable. Maybe I will go shopping with a strange man after all. Once in my room, I attempt to tidy up for some touring. I look at my appearance in the small mirror. *Good Lord. I look nothing like that flawless person who left the States.* I dig into my carry-on, grab some lipstick, and apply it. I sigh. It will have to do. Then I get a whiff of my ruined outfit. I take out my perfume and spray it on. At least that worked. I plop my straw hat back on my messy hair, straighten my shoulders, and try to look like I have it all together as I head back to the lobby. As soon as my dear Big Red is back in my possession, I will have clean clothes and feel more like myself.

Before any sightseeing can begin I need something before I puke, *again*, this time in the car or, God forbid, in some holy temple. I did pack Dramamine way back when, but it won't do me any good because it's in Big Red, who is currently somewhere in outer space circling Earth. Except for the perfume and lipstick, my carry-on is becoming more useless by the minute.

I wonder what people here take to alleviate nausea. I'll take anything I can get. Off to the pharmacy.

CHAPTER TEN

Squatter anxiety, cannabis, and barking dogs

"There is this to be said for walking: It's the one mode of human locomotion by which a man proceeds on his own two feet, upright, erect, as a man should be, not squatting on his rear haunches like a frog."
~ Edward Abbey

May 7, Paro, Bhutan

The highlight today is the National Museum, high in the mountains. The warm temperature and long drive don't play well with my already messed-up stomach. It's stop and go all the way on the one-lane road. If that's not enough, I'm sitting in the back of a vehicle that jerks every time Dawa changes gears. My nausea gets worse by the minute. While I was waiting in the hotel lobby, another guest told me that wherever I am heading, there will be a bend in the road "once every nine seconds." Knowing this in advance helps, but I'd kill for a saltine cracker to assuage my churning stomach. I take deep breaths, determined not to let a little motion sickness get in the way of today's long-anticipated adventures.

Approaching the museum, I marvel at the building and massive buttressed walls. Shaped like a conch shell, intricately painted wooden eaves and cornices adorn the rooftop and windows. I can see why it's considered an architectural wonder.

With its white exterior and red roof, I realize that this is the building I saw as my plane descended. My guide tells me that this type of woodwork facade is common in Bhutan. Formally a fortified monastery called the Paro Dzong, it is one of the oldest and most celebrated in the country.

Getting out of the car, I take in the panoramic view of Paro against the backdrop of the Himalayas, hypnotized by its beauty. A queasy stomach can't dull the awe factor. Turning toward the museum I see an ancient watchtower surrounded by a mosaic of brilliant, colorful flowers. It feels as if you're walking into an Impressionist painting.

Entering, we walk clockwise through the building because of its religious significance. There are six floors of galleries full of a rich variety of artifacts depicting the history and culture of Bhutan. Strolling through, I admire the ancient weapons and shields, religious costumes, and ritual objects dating back to the 1600s. Fascinated by the handicrafts that reflect the daily life here, I find myself obsessing over their detail. My attention turns to some drawings representing Buddhist beliefs and a balcony that houses spectacular paintings of Bhutan's saints and teachers. They serve as a record and guide for contemplative experiences. Most are painted but a few are made of pure silk. I reach out, wishing I could feel the texture between my fingers. The imagery is incredible. Yeshey tells me some of the stories. One of the most revered saints is the Guru Rinpoche. Legend has it he first appeared as an eight-year-old child floating on a lotus blossom, and some regard him as a second Buddha.

Ascending a staircase, we enter the Bhutanese stamp gallery. On display are three-dimensional stamps, ones made of silk, and a stamp depicting Yeti, also known as Big Foot. The Bhutanese believe in the Yeti. Sounds like we have something in common here: Loch Ness Monster, Abominable Snowman, and more recently, Goat Man.

Removing my shoes as is the custom, I enter a chapel that

holds the Tree of Wisdom. A three-dimensional, four-sided, clay carving that depicts the history of Buddhism, its schools and lineages. Taking photos is not allowed inside, which is not a problem because we all know where my cameras are—inside the missing Big Red.

Yeshey does an excellent job of sharing the history surrounding the museum and is kind enough to give me time to take notes in my journal. I must look like I feel. Bone tired and holding on to what little is left in my stomach. With a soft smile, he looks at me, concerned. "Perhaps you would like to return to the hotel and get some rest. Maybe delay our trip to Tiger's Nest Monastery until tomorrow."

Relieved and grateful, I nod. "Yes, please."

On our walk to the car, he points to the foliage along either side of the road. "Do you know what this is?"

"No, but the leaves are quite beautiful."

He laughs, clearly enjoying telling me it's cannabis. "It grows everywhere and is more common than grass. It grows on roadsides, in gardens and vegetable patches, on sports fields, in the forests, and even in sidewalk cracks. You will see it everywhere."

"Is this why Bhutan is considered the happiest place on the planet?" I ask.

Again he laughs. "The locals don't smoke it; they feed it to the livestock. Cows don't like it very much, but the pigs are hooked on it, which is a good thing, because it makes them fat. This is the only country in the world where pigs fly."

I ponder the fact that marijuana is supposed to relieve nausea. Perhaps I should pick a few leaves, take them back to the hotel, and roll a joint, dried or not. Now that would be an adventure!

As we near the car, my GI tract starts making some unpleasant announcements. My first day in Shangri-La and my body feels assaulted from top to bottom. I need to find a bathroom, and soon. I'm hopeful that once I go, I will eliminate one problem. Yeshey points to a cement wall a short distance up a grass hill. I bite my lower lip. I look at him, then at the cement wall. *Please God, don't make it as repulsive as an outhouse.*

I start up the dirt path and stop short, remembering the toilet paper warning: always have it with you because there will be none in the bathrooms. We all know where my stash of toilet paper is.

Going back down the hill, I can see Yeshey is clearly amused that I won't go near a bathroom without tp. Unsure if I can make it back to the hotel without an accident, I tell him I have some tissues in my purse, which is with the driver. He calls him on his cell phone, and Dawa immediately appears, tissues in hand. Sweating bullets, I run up the hill watching two local women vanish around the wall. I get closer. I gag. The smell is overpowering; but when you gotta go, you gotta go, so, holding my breath, I hope this will be a quick trip. On entering, I gasp. *No toilets.* Just three disgusting holes in the ground with no doors or partitions for privacy. Two are currently occupied by a pair of chatting women in squat position. I shift my stare to the empty, totally uninviting hole, all the while trying to figure out my next move. I notice one worn footprint on either side, along with remains of what didn't make it down the hole. Years of squatters have passed through here. I put my hand over my mouth and nose.

I'm faced with a choice: squat over a hole or take my chances until we find a real toilet. Only one decision makes sense to me. Quickly executing an about-face, I carefully sidestep all the human leftovers and get back down the hill. I let out a huge breath and boldly announce: "I can't do it. I just can't squat over a hole. Is there a toilet close by?" Yeshey replies that we are miles from one. "What do you do?" I ask faintly.

"I go outside like everyone else," he replies.

I have no idea why I never gave this toilet situation more thought. Yes, I was told to bring toilet paper, but I don't recall any of my travel books covering the actual toilet facilities. If I'd known before I left home, I would have practiced my squatter skills. If only. Knowing how anal, pardon the pun, I am about public toilets, this is a real challenge.

As for going outside. Other people might be willing to *do* as the Romans *do,* but I refuse. I must figure out an alternative to the hole and the great outdoors. As eager as I am to follow a Buddhist path, this isn't the one I had in mind.

I have only one thought as we head back to the car: *Please Dawa, get me to the hotel as fast as you can.*

Relieved in more ways than one, and desperate for a nap before dinner, I lie down on my first real bed since I left the States. Dropping into a fitful sleep, my mind wanders to my spotless bathrooms (all four of them) back home. Each one is cleaned top to bottom several times a week. I take extra care when I know people are coming over, scrubbing like mad, spraying scent around, checking and double-checking before their arrival. Sometimes I even put a flower in a vase in each bathroom and light a candle, just for effect. I think about the public restrooms I've negotiated in my lifetime. I carefully lay tp on the seat, push the handle with a tissue-covered hand, and open the door the same way. I'm a fanatic about cleanliness. What does this say about my journey on the path to detachment and enlightenment? Well, maybe not detachment. One could say I have been enlightened, however, I seriously doubt this is what the Buddha intended.

May 7 Silver Pine Hotel

Still under the weather, and unable to eat the local cuisine, I request black tea and toast for dinner. Sitting alone, I sip my tea, and once again contemplate picking a few leaves off one of those cannabis plants. If it works for pigs, it might increase my appetite while relieving the nausea. When I finish my light dinner, I join my guide and several other travelers on the hotel patio where a large pit fire is burning. As the sun sets and the evening sky darkens, we head out to the hotel parking lot. An enormous silver disk glimmers in the night. Several dancers wearing spectacular masks and costumes of bright-colored silks

and rich brocades have arrived. They are here to entertain us under the light of the enormous full moon. There are three types of dances, or *chams*: ones with moral themes, celebratory, and those that protect a place from harmful spirits. For almost two hours we watch the dancers perform, pausing only to change into the different costumes and masks unique to each type of dance. I'm thrilled to witness these since chams are typically only performed at spiritual and religious festivals.

The most significant celebration happens in May on the night of the full moon, when Buddhists world-wide celebrate the birth, enlightenment, and death of Buddha more than 2,500 years ago. Known as Buddha Day, it is the most sacred day on their calendar, and I am here. Bathed in the light of the moon, I'm filled with unimaginable joy.

May 8, Silver Pine Hotel

No one told me about the barking dogs!

I woke up feeling out of sorts and edgy. My muscles are tense, and my ears echo with the sound of barking dogs. At first, I thought it was just an isolated incident. Perhaps it was the full moon that set them off. *Not!* I was told at breakfast—another round of black tea and toast—that there are about 10,000 dogs in Bhutan. Buddhists here do not believe in putting them in shelters or getting them fixed. They run wild through the streets of every town and village. They sleep by day, but at night they run in packs and bark, and bark, and bark. They even get into a rhythm where they all stop just long enough to make you think the cacophony is over. But then you hear one bark, and another concert begins. "You should always bring earplugs," I'd been told, and I did. Want to guess where they are?

Here's another tidbit about dogs. In addition to being man's best friend, dogs hold a special religious status in Buddhism. Buddhists believe that within the world of animals, dogs have the best chance to be reborn as humans. So they are respected and treated quite well—all 10,000 of them. On that note, I guess the lesson is, tolerance and acceptance of things that drive me crazy.

In the overall scheme of things, it appears that not having clean clothes is becoming less important when compared to having to choose between smelly pit holes or the great outdoors for the execution of my private business. Not great options if you ask me. Of course, there is no choice involved when it comes to the barking dogs. I'm beginning to think *perfectly planned* needs to be removed from my playlist along with some of my *must-haves* since I still don't have any of my all-important stuff. Where the hell is Big Red?

CHAPTER ELEVEN

Imprisoned by Perfectionism and Routine

All my tedious planning and packing for this journey took more than nine months. This trip has been a lifetime in the making. I am addicted to the pursuit of perfectionism. I diligently seek it everywhere. In an attempt to feel better about it, I acknowledge that everyone has some sort of addiction—after all, my choice could have been much worse: alcohol, drugs, food, or smoking. But it can be just as debilitating. Perfectionism has all the attributes of any addiction. It is a self-imposed prison that destroys your ability to be in harmony with the flow of life. I find no consolation in knowing we perfectionist types have been around since the beginning of time.

I'm a failure at letting go of the idea that perfection will result in the sense of peace and comfort I've sought since childhood. As far back as I can remember, I equated perfectionism with being in total control of everyone, and everything. So far, I've been quite successful in blurring the lines between what is real, what is truth, and what is just an illusion.

My attempts to be the perfect homemaker, mother, spouse, nurse, business woman, and teacher; maintaining a perfect personal appearance, and home, were necessary to validate that image of who I want to be. I created an impossible world, and the results rarely match the goal. It is exhausting trying to be perfect. I believed that being perfect came with payoffs and benefits, and that the result of my efforts would lead to nothing but the best of outcomes in my life.

Right alongside this craziness was the extraordinary effort I put into maintaining my numerous daily routines. Morning routines, afternoon routines, evening routines, and special weekend routines, all rigidly kept. I'd become a slave to them, and I've often considered what it would take to let go of this need for perfect order in my life. More Buddha books? More meditation? More therapy?

These issues come up quite frequently in my weekly sessions with Lisa, my therapist. There were plenty of examples from which to choose. One was how I take the word *routine* to a whole new level when grocery shopping. When entering the store, I always start with aisle one, then two, and so on, always going in the same direction down each aisle. Skipping an aisle or going in the opposite direction was unthinkable. Backtracking for something I forgot was impossible. And I can't even begin to explain how pissed off I'd get if I walked into *my* grocery store and things had been rearranged. Not only would I have to relearn the location of everything, I would have to reconfigure the order of my coupons, because now my Fiber One cereal coupon would no longer line up with the top shelf of aisle four. I was aware of my grocery store fixation but was convinced it saved me time. I knew exactly where I was going, and how to get there, so it was easy to justify my behavior.

Then Lisa gave me a homework assignment. Go to the store and totally mix it up. I thought, *how hard can this be, going down aisle four before aisle three?* The next time I pointed my cart in a whole new direction, convinced I could do this with ease. Mix it up I did. I felt nsettled and rattled as I tried to locate items. I was frustrated, stressed, and tired by the time I left the store, because that whole mixing-it-up thing had added an hour to the shopping trip, an hour that was not part of my routine, and a perfect routine was my *everything*.

With practice, I finally mastered letting go of my rigidity when it comes to grocery shopping. But a lot more work would be required on so many other fronts as perfectionism and routine are still prevalent in my life. The stage was set long ago for one fiasco to follow another from the moment I announced "I'm going to the Himalayas." It was as if the Universe was both testing and laughing at me, determined to obstruct more than nine months of arduous planning, preparation, and packing perfection. This trip has been a lifetime in the making.

CHAPTER TWELVE

The arrival of Big Red and the trek to Tiger's Nest

May 8, Tiger's Nest Monastery, Paro, Bhutan

The good news is my bags have arrived. There she is, Big Red in all her glory, waiting for me at the airport along with the bulging gray duffel bag I had packed on the floor at JFK. I can't wait to change out of the clothes I've been wearing for four days.

I push Big Red over to the restroom only to discover she won't fit through the door. I struggle to turn her sideways and squeeze her through, but after several tries I admit defeat. For the first time, reality strikes: I will replay this battle again, and again over the next few weeks as I travel with a suitcase that weighs almost as much as I do.

Dragging Red over to where Yeshey and Dawa are waiting, I can't find the tiny piece of paper with the combination for the lock. A struggle ensues on the floor of yet another airport terminal. When none of us can open that friggin three-dollar lock, we have only one option left: break it. Yeshey talks to an airport official who fetches a hammer and bangs on the lock until it opens. Inside Big Red, I'm greeted by a rainbow of colored dots on top, in between, and underneath the contents. Apparently my genius idea of putting my pills into plastic containers wasn't so great. They were no match for the rough handling and abuse baggage takes. Frustrated, I think of all the time and forethought I wasted on packaging those 484 damned pills. I can feel my face get hot as the four of us stare at the colorful array of pills sprinkled everywhere. They either think this is some strange American custom or that I have a drug problem. And what must onlookers think about the spectacle of two Bhutanese men in the middle of the Paro airport kneeling beside an American woman as she digs through an obscenely large suitcase? I scoop up as many of the pills as I can and shove them into a side pocket of the suitcase. I will worry about organizing them later.

To my chagrin, the pills are not the worst of my problems. Pulling out one of my cutest tops, I discover a gooey mess—Woolite found, and not in the bottle. You know those little plastic bottles with the tight lids made for traveling? Take my advice, they don't work. Heading out of the terminal I wonder how many more outfits have succumbed to the spilled Woolite? My perfectly planned and efficiently packed suitcase is unraveling at the seams.

Changing in the bathroom, I avoid looking at the unsightly hole in the floor. We leave the airport and head to the legendary Taktsang Goemba—the Tiger's Nest Monastery. Actually a series of thirteen monasteries, it perches precariously on the edge of a cliff, 10,000 feet above Paro. One of the most sacred Buddhist sites, visitors from the outside world are required to get special permission and a guide.

On the drive there, Yeshey briefs me on the trek ahead. The trail has three stages. The first one ends at the Taktsang Teahouse, where we will stop for some light snacks. Once we reach the third stage, we will have an excellent view of the Taktsang Monastery. To get inside, we will tackle stairs that first descend, then ascend.

At the start of the first trail, you have the option of going all the way up by foot, which can take several hours depending on your fitness, or you can travel partway by mule. A risk taker, I decide to ride a mule despite my disastrous experiences at riding horses.

A young boy brings over a mule named Mindu. She looks old and harmless, but one never knows. I take in a deep breath, put my foot in the stirrup, and swing my leg over. I pat her side and say a silent prayer. *May I be safe.* Because donkeys kick when they get scared I add, *May you not be afraid.*

Before we start out, Yeshey points upward. My eyes widen. The monastery looks like a tiny speck perched on the edge of a cliff, rising above the wispy clouds. It's hard to fathom how such a place can be reached on foot. I'm anxious to get started. Saddled up, my guide walks in front leading the way.

It's nerve-wracking how close Mindu tends to walk near the edge. If it crumbles, even slightly, or she loses her footing and slips, my *trip of a lifetime* could come to a sudden end. Despite this, I try to concentrate on the tranquility of my surroundings, the sound of rushing water from the mountain streams, accompanied by the ringing of the giant prayer wheels turning in the water. I soak in the breathtaking vistas as the trail weaves through beautiful blue pine and oak forests. Spanish moss hangs from the trees that are filled with clusters of brilliant red, green, blue, and yellow prayer flags that flutter in the cool breeze. They look like celestial laundry.

I'm amazed at the number of chortens on the mountain side of the trail. We saw young monks and pilgrims building these mini temples on our trek and passed locals selling handheld prayer wheels, strings of beads, temple bells, and the like. Symbols of reverence mark the trail. I spot an older man leaning against a tree, holding his walking stick. I do a double take when I realize the top of his stick looks like the head of a penis. Shaking my head, I'd ask Yeshey about it but don't want to offend him.

Chortens (*an offering*) are built to honor significant religious

figures, monks, and deceased loved ones. Some are located in places to ward off demons, such as the ones at crossroads, bridges, and mountain passes. Building a chorten is considered beneficial and creates positive karma. An important element of a chorten is the tree of life, a wooden pole with thousands of mantras, or prayers covering it, and placed in its center during a ceremony.

Ninety minutes later we reach the rest stop. Here we leave

Mindu behind as animals can go no farther. She has been a perfect ride. I wait outside the partially covered pavilion as Yeshey goes into the teahouse. The sun is shining in a crystal clear blue sky. I choose a place to sit and let the rays envelop me. Tearing up, I'm overcome by indescribable emotion as I gaze at my surroundings. It feels so surreal to be here after all the months of planning. *At last,* I think, *I am actually living my dream.* I feel blessed and at peace. With a deep sense of gratitude, I silently give thanks. I snap out of my blissful reverie as Yeshey sits down beside me and hands me a cup of black tea. He points at several white buildings with the familiar red roofs. Built into the rock face, this is the best spot for an unobstructed view of the Taktsang Monastery. Even from a distance, it is majestic. As I take a sip of tea, he tells me the legend of the Tiger's Nest Monastery.

Its construction dates to the eighth century and a man called Guru Rinpoche. Revered as the second reincarnated Buddha, he brought Buddhism from Tibet to Bhutan. He arrived at Tiger's Nest flying on the back of a tigress who brought him to this sheer cliff face. He meditated in a cave that became the spot where the monastery was built. His meditation resulted in the conversion of the people of Paro to Buddhism.

It's time to continue our journey. We are at the halfway point now, and it's all on foot from here. I watch people descending the trail, huffing and puffing. Smugly I think they look unfit. I feel confident in my ability to do this climb. Ego will get you every time, and so will wearing inappropriate footwear for a hike such as this. But I must say, I do look fashionable wearing my straw hat with the black ribbon and cute little Velcro sneakers.

Ascending the precarious trail, you cannot look ahead or left or right. Each step must be carefully calculated. My heart feels as if it's going to pump itself right out of my chest, causing me to stop every few feet. Shocked to realize how physically unfit I am, I wish I'd clocked a few more days at the gym. There are no level areas along the path, so even while resting you must be on your guard. It takes almost two hours to walk the rest of the way up. Later, I learn that my physical state has less to do with being out of shape or my cute little sneakers. My difficulty, like that of the others, was adjusting to the altitude. Monks, along with an occasional woman with a child strapped to her back, easily pass us, expending no effort whatsoever because they're accustomed to the high altitude.

The monastery is not visible for most the climb because of all the vegetation, but once we are in a clearing, we can see the monastery jutting out along a steep precipice as it clings to the near-vertical side of the cliff. I rest for a moment, awestruck by its astonishing size and how it seems to defy gravity. I wonder about the logistics. The fortitude it took to build and then rebuild after a devastating fire in 1998. How many lives were lost in the effort? Ascending once again, you can spot the Taktsang Tea House through the trees and prayer flags below. We will stop there once more on our descent.

Several times as we continue, Yeshey reaches out to steady me before I take a tumble. I utter a faint thank-you to him and Buddha. Ninety minutes later we reach the final stage of our climb.

Tiger's Nest isn't the only thing you can see from this dramatic location. Jammed into the narrow crags of the rock face are some smaller buildings. One, Snow Lion Cave, is a meditation retreat perched in a narrow crevice. If you don't mind heights, this would be a unique place to meditate. A forty-year-old monk intends to stay in seclusion here for more than three years. He will repeat this three times in his lifetime. I imagine myself doing this and coming down from the mountain fully enlightened until the image of me crippled after thirty minutes in the full lotus position flashes through my mind. I think I'll pass.

We cross a bridge over a waterfall that thunders beneath us before dropping 200 feet into a sacred pool. Glancing up, I spot some of the red-robed monks who live, pray, and maintain the temples here. Is this an adrenaline rush I feel, or is it the altitude?

The last part of the trail is a long flight of stairs—800 to be exact—that descend to a bridge and then ascend again all the way to the monastery. To make matters worse, some of the steps are crumbling. I tread carefully. I hold tight to the railings with both hands to support myself in case I fall. Like a kid, I want to ask are we there yet, but I'm too out of breath. There are places with no railings where tourists have toppled over the edge. I think about the worst-case scenario. My knuckles turn white. Some steps are quite high. I gather what little strength I have left and pull myself up. When we get to our destination, the sweet smell of incense fills the air. There is an aura that surrounds the monastery. It's strange, but I feel lighter, my breath less labored. It must be this sacred place.

Four main temples with white-washed facades and red roofs topped with golden apexes make up the monastery. Looking out over the Paro Valley, we can see how the structures adapt to the nature of the rocky ledges. Removing our shoes, we enter the main cave—there are eight in all—through a narrow passageway. A dozen images of Bodhisattvas (people motivated by compassion who are seeking enlightenment) are displayed here, each surrounded by flickering butter lamps. In an adjoining small cell, there is a sacred scripture written with ink made from gold dust and the crushed bone of a divine lama.

Within the monastery are several small, elaborately decorated chapels. Painted on the walls are deities with animal heads. In one chapel, a rock image of a goddess is hidden in a hole in the floor. The largest chapel holds several large, golden statues encrusted with precious and semiprecious jewels. Offerings of rice, crackers, cookies, water, and money lay scattered around the statues. Yeshey hands me a few coins. With gratitude I make my offering.

We enter a small, lower chapel that houses a dark, cold cave. Inside is an altar behind a spectacular gilded door. This is where the Guru Rinpoche spent three months meditating. By doing this, he protected the valley from all evil spirits. I am told that some have felt a cold breath coming from the cave.

As we wander through the chapels, I realize something interesting. Aware of the differences between Catholicism and Buddhism, I am starting to recognize how the physical structures of the two also support those differences.

When we've finished our tour, we set out on our return trip.

Going down is not as taxing, but each step must still be well thought out. It's like having brakes on both feet. There are times I just go sliding because my toes can no longer hold their grip in my Velcro sneakers without treads. Thankfully, Yeshey is close enough to catch me.

Before our final descent, we stop again at the Taktsang Tea-house for traditional cuisine served buffet-style. There are lots of carbohydrates such as potatoes and rice to replenish what you lost along the trail. While he remains inside chatting with some friends, I take my lunch of crackers and black tea outside. I'm still a little under the weather, but there's another reason for my sparse fare. After all, the less you eat, the less you go. I shift in my seat at the thought of squatting over a hole or, even worse, squatting in the woods.

With my hands curled around my cup of steaming-hot tea, I gaze at the stunning landscape, perhaps for the last time. Tiger's Nest Monastery, constructed in 1692 at dizzying heights, should be on everyone's bucket list. My mind begins to wander. I think about how far I am from home. I wonder what time it is there and what my husband, family, and friends are doing right now. Are they eating, sleeping, watching TV, or maybe on their computers? Are they driving to work on crowded, noise-polluted streets or shopping at big box stores? Smiling, I don't miss any of it. A warmth circulates through my body as I sit in the beauty of this silence. I am in the land of happiness, and I'm beginning to see it, breathe it, touch it.

CHAPTER THIRTEEN

They're back!

May 9, Thimpu, Bhutan

This morning as I repack Big Red, I think about the courteous staff at the Silver Pine Hotel where I would return to spend my last night in Paro before my trip to Nepal. I'm not sure the staff will be happy to see me return. There are no elevators, and it took two men, one in the front and one in the back, to carry Big Red up and down three flights of winding stairs. Since they know I am coming back, they would be wise to stick me on the first floor. For a moment, I consider lightening the load, but that's all I ever do about Big Red.

With Dawa driving, we leave Paro and head to Thimpu, the capital of Bhutan. We come to a pine-covered hillside bisected by a cluster of white prayer flags on huge vertical bamboo poles being erected by dozens of locals. Someone has died, and the 108 prayer flags will assist the spirit of the deceased on its journey to its next reincarnation. The number 108 is considered sacred by some Eastern religions with many interpretations. I remember one from my readings. One stands for God or higher Truth, zero stands for emptiness or completeness in spiritual practice, and eight stands for infinity or eternity. Stopping to watch as the people silently go about their task, their reverence for the dead is unmistakable. Death here seems like a community event, natural in the cycle of existence.

As we get deeper into the mountains, Dawa stops and we view the endless rows of tiny clay *stupas* (shrines) tucked into the crevices on the mountain face. Stupas play a significant role in funerals. After a person dies, a ceremony is performed in front of an image of the deceased. A lama reads from sacred texts, and the picture of the deceased is burned. The ashes are then mixed with clay and formed into tiny conical shapes. Sometimes bone fragments are taken from the skull of the dead person and mixed in as well. Marking the landscape as another blessing for a loved one who has died, they become a receptacle for sacred power.

My thoughts turn to how we say good-bye to our loved ones back home and the funeral industry with its extravagant coffins and huge headstones that we select although our dearly departed are unable to appreciate the time and expense. And all the minutiae—a guest book, prayer cards that people throw away, and flowers, all those flowers. And while our loved ones might be remembered by a few, the Bhutanese pay homage to all departed loved ones, known and unknown, each time they pass those prayer flags and rows and rows of tiny stupas dotting the mountain ranges. I have read much about the Western fear of death and dying. Buddhists are taught that death is a natural part of life and not something to fear. Death isn't final; it's merely something that leads to a person's eventual rebirth. That doesn't mean they don't grieve—grief is universal—but how wonderful not to fear death, knowing your spirit will seek out a new life and a new body: another opportunity for self-improvement. You have to love that.

The two-hour drive to Thimpu is an experience. The narrow road snakes around blind turns alongside a sheer abyss that drops off just a foot or two from the side of our car. If this isn't heart-stopping enough, vehicles large and small are coming from the opposite direction every few minutes. The trip is underscored by the sound of Dawa blasting his car horn every few feet to warn cars coming around the next blind turn of our presence and hopefully preventing a head-on collision that could send us plunging 3,000 feet. He says it's all part of driving here. I'm told that some vehicles have taken the plunge, thus adding a few more little stupas to the landscape. Of course, that immediately brings to mind this quote from Helen Keller: "A bend in the road is not the end of the road… unless you fail to make the turn."

Tearing my thoughts away from impending doom, I realize the scenery is charming. Passing barley and wheat fields where farmers are drying their harvest along the roadside, I see a temple on a hill, accessible by a suspension footbridge over-looking the river. I love the apple orchards, the neat-looking haystacks, and the farmhouses with rooftops decorated with bright-red chilies. Finally, we pass through the security check-point marking the entry to Thimpu, the capital of Bhutan.

We arrive at the Riverview Hotel, and as they hand me my key, I pray there is an elevator. I wonder what will happen if there comes a time when there isn't one, and I'm left to my own devices to maneuver Big Red. Relieved that I don't have to answer that yet, I enter my room and open Red.

When I'm traveling, no matter how short my stay, I like to

nest and unpack. Wanting to hang up my clothes, I discover that there are a total of five hangers in the closet. The room and the bathroom are small, so I spread my makeup and hair care products, curling iron, blow-dryer, and Waterpik out on the windowsills and bedside table. My nesting complete, I gaze at all my belongings, and the contradiction between how I want to be, and how I choose to be strikes me once again. In hindsight, I will realize the signs should have shown me what really matters, especially in the land of simplicity.

Meeting up with Yeshey, we head out for a warm, sunny stroll through Thimpu. It may be the biggest city in Bhutan, but you can easily walk the whole thing in less than a day. Quaint, it has some cafés, restaurants, art stores, and souvenir shops sprinkled around the main thoroughfare. The buildings—by law—reflect the same traditional Bhutanese-style architecture. We walk in and out of shops that sell decorative masks, carpets, jewelry, and

an array of wooden products. The shopkeepers are warm and friendly and answer my questions in soft voices. I take note of the tourists I see casually dressed in jeans, t-shirts, visors, and baseball caps. Yes, there is a requirement to dress modestly, but I am clearly overdressed in my expensive sundress and matching hat. I have the entire Estée Lauder line on my face, hair perfectly curled and held in place by so much hair spray even the wind of a thousand prayer flags couldn't move a strand. Somehow my desire to commune with the locals is overshadowed by my attire, not to mention the time it takes for me to get ready each day. Hundreds of pigeons cover the square. I grimace as I struggle to plant my designer sandals on something other than their droppings.

I'm amazed at the amount of construction going on. They use intricately woven bamboo for scaffolding on buildings of all heights.

We stop to watch a group of boys and one girl putting together a wall. The boys are on top of it, pounding the mud and singing together in unison, while the girl is barefoot on the ground, knee-deep in mud, scraping away at the sides of the wall with her bare hands. It won't be the first wall in the making that we will pass. You decide who is having the easier time of it.

Our destination leads us to the Changlimithang grounds, where

an audience is cheering on a group of men engaged in an archery tournament. The Bhutanese are passionate about their national pastime known as *Dha*. I'm told that archery matches are among the most colorful events in this country. Their traditional archery equipment consists of a long bamboo bow, but most archers use state-of-the-art bows. We sit and watch a match made up of five men on each side. There are small wooden targets placed at such a long distance that team members need to stand dangerously close to them and yell back how well their teammate performed. As we listen to their howling and chanting, I'm tempted to stand up and cheer. Whenever a target is hit, it's followed by a ceremonial song and dance, all part of the game. Unlike Western fans who taunt the team that doesn't score, the Bhutanese dance for joy no matter which side they are on. This might be another reason they are the happiest people on Earth. Some food for thought for all you sport fanatics.

According to tradition, women must not touch an archer's bow, and if an archer sleeps with a woman the night before a tournament, his performance will be affected. I guess they have to make some serious decisions about which target they want to master!

Leaving the Changlimithang grounds, we encounter thousands of prayer flags strung across narrow bridges as far as the eye can see. Inscribed with sacred emblems, symbols, and mantras, they represent prayers for good fortune, health, happiness, and protection. They flutter in front of homes, hotels, shops and temples, on rooftops, bridges, and in fields of red rice—everywhere. An important part of life and Buddhism, they send their prayers to heaven. What beautiful, expressive messengers.

Continuing our walk through Thimpu, I stop to listen to the moving chanting of monks from one of the remote Buddhist monasteries. I close my eyes, savoring the experience.

At an altitude of 8,000 feet, it's population of about 98,000 makes Thimpu the only place in Bhutan large enough to call a city. With only a couple of main streets, it lacks even a single traffic light. A few years ago one was installed and quickly dismantled after the locals complained that it was too impersonal. We pause near two traffic circles where I watch a police officer, standing on a wooden pedestal, direct cars. His hand gestures are as graceful as a dancer's. Traffic jams here are not caused by cars, but by slow-walking livestock mooing and bleating. Each car patiently waits its turn. There is a total absence of road rage because it's highly unlikely a honking horn or shout would be enough to get a cow or goat to move any faster. It's just another reminder of the uniqueness of this place, where even driving is dramatically different.

They are currently building a gold-covered Buddha that will stand 153 feet tall and face the Himalayas. It will house more than 100,000 small Buddhas. I envision myself gazing at this massive Buddha, its gold surface glittering against the blue sky overlooking the Thimpu Valley. But its beauty will not be the only thing that tugs at my heart. Its purpose is to radiate energy and bestow blessings, peace, and happiness to the whole world. I think about the moral conduct of Buddhism, built on love and compassion for all sentient beings. How different our lives would be if we had a more Buddha-like nature. I love this religion with all its textures. *Perhaps*, I think, sighing, *I will need to make a return trip to see this*.

Returning to the hotel, the day comes to an end. Too tired to go down to dinner, I order room service. Throwing caution to the wind, I decide to be daring and order some chicken broth with my dry toast and black tea. So far, the gods have been with me, and I haven't had to squat over the hole when we've been out and about. I'm praying my luck will last. Bound and determined to sidestep the squat, I plan on being strategic when I begin to eat more.

Drifting off to sleep, I'm a little more at peace with this way of life. Perhaps I could be happy here. As long as I had a modern bathroom, that is. What strikes me most is the manner in which these people go about their daily business with such ease and contentment. Never rushing, they seem to enjoy all facets of their lives. Living in the moment, time is not their enemy. They are kind and generous people who have reverence for all sentient beings—including cows, goats, pigeons, and of course, barking dogs.

May 10, Riverview Hotel, Thimpu, Bhutan

I have risen, but I'm not shining. They're back. Another round of those damned dogs. This is torture. As soon as the sun goes down, all it takes is one howl, and like a prayer flag catching the wind, it sends all the dogs into a frenzy. They don't stop barking until daybreak, which explains why every, and I mean every, dog you see is out cold during the day. You could wave a yak burger under their noses, and they wouldn't budge. A set of earplugs, along with pieces of tissue in my ears, and a pillow over my head offered no relief last night. I wanted to reach for the Ambien, but sleeping pills can decrease respiratory function and result in a worsening of symptoms at high altitudes. At some point, I must decide: will it be death by Ambien or barking dogs.

As I prepare for today's adventure, it dawns on me that even halfway around the world I can't seem to escape the havoc created by these four-legged creatures we call our *furry friends.*

CHAPTER FOURTEEN

The perfect storm

"Dogs are the leaders of the planet. If you see two life forms, one of them is making a poop, the other one is carrying it for him, who would you assume is in charge?"
~ Jerry Seinfeld

Combine my insistence that everything be planned to perfection with the trappings of my materialistic life, and the result will likely be *shit happens*.

In 2007, my husband and I moved into a beautiful, new condo complex situated on 80 acres of land. We selected a location that would capture the morning sunrise and the early sunset. I wanted to create a perfect space to rejuvenate and renew my mental well-being and provide me with a personal sanctuary. It would support my continued commitment to the inner peace I have strived for my whole life. I wanted family and friends to experience a feeling of warmth and tranquility on entering our new home. To accomplish this, I selected each piece of decor with that goal in mind.

I insisted that everything be white, white, and whiter than white. After months of investing careful thought, and a ton of energy, I had created what I thought was the perfect inner sanctum both visually and psychologically. The irony was that this 3,000-square-foot beast did anything but soothe my soul.

Enter Lenny, Oscar, and Lulu Bell.

I eagerly anticipated our first Thanksgiving in our new home, planning a huge family dinner to show off my new, untouched, unmarked, extremely white, perfect home. Because both my adult children live in Boston, it would be the first time they would see it. The curtains rise, scene one: Daughter Michele arrived first, with Lulu Bell, her toy Chihuahua. In less than five minutes darling Lulu left me two unwanted *house-warming* presents. She had pooped and peed in my brand-new, previously pristine, inner sanctum. As the weekend progressed Lulu— supposedly house-trained on pee-pee pads—was squatting and peeing wherever and whenever. Her's was not the type of spirit intended to foster peace and harmony.

Enter son, Michael, and girlfriend, Louise, with Lenny and Oscar, their dachshunds. They assured me that both dogs were perfectly house-trained and that they never had accidents inside. It wouldn't be long before scene two of the perfect storm began.

As soon as the turkey and all the trimmings were ready, we sat down to eat. Sparing no time for the traditional prayer, this hungry crowd had only one thing on their minds: food. I on the other hand gratefully took in the heartwarming picture of my family gathered in my perfect home, the sun casting its rays on us. Slowly, my eyes followed the sunlight bouncing off the glass windows onto my shiny hardwood floor. My gaze landed on a large mound of something brownish in color under the couch. I glanced twice and then squinted, thinking, *It can't be. It's probably just one of the dog's stuffed toys, a loose sock that one of them confiscated, or a piece of rawhide.*

No one noticed me head into the next room. Stopping short, I quickly realized that *it* wasn't a sock or a stuffed toy, nor some rawhide. Disgusted yet trying to be discreet, I calmly walked into the kitchen, grabbed a bunch of paper towels, went back into my beautiful sunlit room, and scooped up that mound. Heading straight for the front door, I tossed the offensive package outside.

Ron, my husband, had apparently been following my action. "Ellie, you can't just throw that out the door. Someone will step in it."

Forks paused in midair as everyone turned toward me. So much for discretion and trying to hide the nasty. I raised both arms in the air in a questioning pose and said, "Excuse *me*? Did you actually say poop doesn't belong outside, but it's perfectly okay in the house? What's wrong with this picture?" Nobody said a word; they all continued eating. By the end of the day, I felt as if I was Linda Blair in *The Exorcist* with my head spinning around as I tried to spot any land mines an unsuspecting guest might step on. By the time the day was over, I was both relieved and grateful that my human and dog guests had all left. Of course, one holiday follows another, and Christmas would bring more stormy weather.

Christmas was a repeat performance, with my dog, Roxie, throwing her bonus pile into the mix. By the end of the day, I was completely exhausted. The dog-gone, doggy deposit situation had dominated my every waking moment.

With no more holidays on the horizon, I went on a crusade to prevent any further besmirching of our home. I hoped to enjoy my perfect oasis, but that wasn't in the cards. Even with those dogs eighty-two miles away, it wasn't over yet.

The day Ron helped me take down the Christmas decorations and dismantle the tree, I was in for a leftover surprise. While I carefully wrapped each ornament, Ron called from across the room, "Oh Ellie, look, a Yule log!" I looked down on the floor where the tree had been. There it was, a nice, elongated, dried-out turd that had been hiding under my expensive, brocade tree skirt. If I wasn't ticked off enough, Ron's next comment just about put me over the edge. "At least, it's easier to pick up now." As I walked away, letting him attend to the *business*, I pondered what made more sense: suicide or murder?

The following September, the kids, along with their three

not-house-trained dogs, came to celebrate my mom's ninetieth birthday. I'd prepared a fabulous dinner for us for the night before. I set the table with my best linens and dinnerware and lit the candles. It looked like a Norman Rockwell painting. We were sitting at the table and had just started the entrée when I noticed, smack-dab in the middle of the floor, you guessed it, a pile of dog poop. Why am I the one who always sees it first? Sadly, this hadn't been the first anointing that evening, but this time, I refused to pick it up. I just sat there and announced, "There is a pile over there. Someone please dispose of it." Nobody moved! For God's sake, *nobody* moved! They just kept eating in silence. How could they keep eating with that piece of crap lying not two feet from the dinner table?

In utter disbelief, I said curtly, "Somebody had better pick that up." Still no one moved. Totally exasperated, I said, "What is this, a barn?" Only then was the silence broken.

"It's not my dog," said my daughter.

"Well, it's not my dog's, either," said my son.

Fed up, I said, "Well, it came out of somebody's dog, so one of you, please pick it up."

My daughter exclaimed, "That's not Lulu's, hers look like a pretzel, and that is *not* a pretzel shape."

Like an idiot, I joined in and said, "Well, it's not my dog's!" With no DNA evidence to back up his claim of non-owner-ship, and his inability to describe what his dog's poop looks like, Michael finally picked it up.

Those dogs were working overtime all weekend. The curtains had risen on another long, unforgettable performance. One that would push me over the edge. Not even the loving kind-ness of Buddha, Shiva, Allah, Mohammad, or God could have forgiven them.

It began with Ron standing over Lenny, yelling at him to get off my beautiful, all-white fireside chair, the one that even my guests are afraid to sit on. When Lenny wouldn't move, Ron went over, and as he pushed him off, Lenny left behind an ocean of bright yellow rippling across the entire seat. I am by nature a reserved person who rarely, if ever, raises my voice or uses foul language. But this time something snapped, and I began to yell at Ron, "Get it off. Get it off; get the f'ing cover off!" Ron was almost successful in calming me down until I watched Lenny, in a state of fright, leap onto and then off of the other all-white chair, leaving behind the *second coming*—another wave of pee streaked across my once fresh and untouched white cushion. I took one look at that dog and somewhere deep inside me all the pent-up stress and anxiety erupted like a flow of hot molten lava, and I released a succession of incoherent, blood-curdling screams.

Meanwhile, trying to escape the fray, Oscar, Lenny's partner in crime, had hightailed it onto my custom-made couch. Still screaming, I turned and was stunned into silence as I watched Oscar, now scared shitless, leave it behind as he jumped off the couch and ran for cover. Ron didn't know what to do or which way to run. I belted out another round of screaming: "*My cushions, my cushions!*"

Ron said abruptly, "Listen, Ellie, why don't we just turn the cushions over?"

This shocked me into a deadly, evil silence. When I found my voice again, I yelled, "Are you God-damn crazy?"

He should have shut up at this point, but no. He had to follow it with "It's just furniture, Ellie, just fabric and wood." At that precise moment, I had only one thought. *Where is that kitchen knife, the new, big, serrated one I bought for our beautiful, calm, serene home? I am going to* **EXPLETIVE DELETED** *kill him.* One would have thought he'd said enough, but he wasn't finished yet. Without missing a beat, he said, "Ellie, look at it this way. It's like breaking in a new car." As I tossed the pee-and-poop stained covers into the washer, my thoughts turned to *heinous ways to murder all three of them in the slowest possible fashion.*

Sadly, there was no end to this nightmarish storm because shortly after that, Michele's precious Lulu Bell decided to take a cue from Mike's dogs and she peed, not once but twice, on my beautiful futon with the fabric that looks like an Impressionist painting. Ron found it the hard way. He sat in it. Ahh, karma at last! I wonder if good old Sid— aka Siddhartha Gautama— would have treated the Dias clan of dogs with love and respect if he had seen them in action today. It would be fair to ask why I wasn't strong enough to stand up to my family and announce, "It's the dogs or me." Or demand that the dogs stay home or get kenneled, or that we pen them. But that's another story.

My perfect condo was supposed to create a sacred space to nurture my spirit. It did anything but. Nothing was safe; nothing was sacred. I should have been *enlightened* by the fact that nothing in life turns out as one expects or demands. You would have thought that I would have learned the folly of my attachment to *my stuff* by the time I began planning my perfect *trip of a lifetime*. One would have thought the holiday debacles would have been a game changer, but as it turns out, learning my lesson on the futility of material attachment would have to wait until I went a few rounds with Big Red.

CHAPTER FIFTEEN

A lama's blessing

May 10, Thimpu, Bhutan

Today we set off to visit the King's Memorial Chorten. Built in 1974 in memory of the third king, at the request of his mother, it dominates the skyline.

From a distance, I see the Tibetan-style spire topping its white dome, its golden tip glistening in the morning sun. The white-washed chorten has an outward flaring of the rounded part that gives it the shape of a vase. We approach an exquisite gate decorated with three slate carvings of Bodhisattvas that represent compassion, knowledge, and power. Once inside, it's like stepping into another world. On an interior wall are three elaborate stone carvings of different Buddhas. I hear the tinkling of bells, thought to be the voice of the Buddha, mixed with people chatting and chanting in the flower gardens ablaze with color.

Inside are four painted annexes. Four massive stone lions sit atop huge pedestals that guard the corners. The annexes house religious paintings of angry-looking Buddhist deities with their female consorts in graphic sexual poses. One annex has a shrine dedicated to the third king. Unlike other chortens that enshrine the remains of kings, this one has only the king's photo.

The memorial serves as a place of daily worship for both young and old. They will spend the entire day circumambulating it clockwise, chanting their daily prayers, their worn mala beads passing between their practiced fingers. Others spin tiny handheld prayer wheels mumbling mantras so quickly they sound like a steady hum. These metal cylinders contain Buddhist texts and have handles that allows them to be spun. We join the line and walk slowly around the chorten several times. I have chanted in yoga class, but I remain silent among these spiritual people. The rhythm and vibrations of their chants wash over me as an energy courses through my body. I feel a release of tension, a sense of weightlessness.

In one area, there are red prayer wheels, several yards high and three to six yards in diameter. They contain copies of the mantra *Om mani padme hum* and may also hold sacred texts. These are used for spreading spiritual blessings for well-being. It's said that all the teachings of the Buddha are contained in this mantra, and it can't be translated into a simple phrase or sentence. You turn the prayer wheels by hand as you walk counterclockwise. Each clockwise turn of the wheel sends hundreds of prayers up toward the snow-capped peaks of the Himalayas. The sound of laughter rings out as children run between the wheels spinning them as they go, making a game of it.

I spend some time among the large prayer wheels mindfully turning them while I send up my prayers of gratitude for this once-in-a-lifetime experience. Some of the women sit near the prayer wheels, spinning and chatting among hordes of pigeons. The birds go unnoticed. At one point two adorable Bhutanese children decide to help me turn the wheels. I smile at them. No

fear of strangers here in the land of happiness. This is also a place for social gatherings, where the women eat, rest, and then resume praying. I sit next to an older, solemn-faced woman and watch as the locals, many of them frail, engage in the prostrations that are part of their religious tradition. Is she resting or disappointed that she is unable to join in? Prostrations are a symbolic laying down of one's ego. Buddhism requires them to do more than finger their mala beads, murmuring prayers or spinning handheld prayer wheels. It's been said that the Bhutanese believe hard work earns merit. They put this into practice with hours of prostrations and circumambulation, sometimes completing as many as 108 a day. I think about engaging in a prostration or two, but the lower half of my body is still aching from the mule ride and my exhausting trek to Tiger's Nest Monastery. If I get down on all fours, I'll be there to stay. Not to mention that for me to lie down my ego would require an infinite number of prostrations.

Leaving the memorial, we climb to the Drubthob Monastery—one of the few surviving convents in Bhutan—which houses about sixty nuns. Once again removing our shoes, we step inside the temple where a ceremony is in progress. We are invited to sit cross-legged on pillows surrounding the temple's altar with the nuns and a dozen or more monks ranging in age from five to fourteen. The nuns sit against one wall of the temple while the young monks sit in the middle in two lines facing each other. The sisters chant prayers while several of the teenage monks pass around snacks and drinks throughout the ceremony. The younger monks are giggling, poking, and pelting each other with their snacks. They throw in the occasional chant between their antics. It still feels spiritually driven despite the relaxed atmosphere. It's a delight to watch. All I can say is *Eat, pray, laugh*. This is my kind of worship!

Toward the end of the prayer session, we go up to the altar where holy water is poured into our palms. Following Yeshey's lead, I brush the holy water across my forehead, then walk behind the altar where we stand in front of a lama sitting in the lotus position on a cushioned throne high above us. Entering the monastery at the age of six to become a monk and now a lama at seventeen, he is already considered a teacher of the Buddhist tradition. The lama ties a knot in a thin red cord called a protection-and-blessing cord, prays over it, blows the power of his mantra onto it, and bowing, gracefully places it around Yeshey's neck. I am also blessed. As we step outside the temple, Yeshey, who now has two red cords around his neck, tells me the cords are symbolic of the lama's blessing, which continues to protect you even after you leave his presence. He lets me in on a secret: "Attending this traditional Buddhist ceremony and being given this blessing is extremely rare for tourists." I beam.

What an unexpected gift. Outside, the midday air is so clear we have a fantastic view of Tashichhodzong, which was built as a Buddhist monastery. Considered another jewel of Bhutanese architecture, it now houses important branches of local government and is home to the throne room and offices of the king. Next door is the king's palace surrounded by lush, terraced fields. We continue our walk down the hill to Thimpu's Centenary Farmers Market, which is held outdoors each weekend, rain or shine. Here residents take a break from whatever they are doing to catch up on the week's gossip and buy fresh fruits, vegetables, and a lot more. They travel from all over to sell their products. The market is as much of a staple in their lives as prayer and is considered *the* most important shopping event.

The spacious, two-story market houses more than 400 roofed stalls. Designed with beautiful marble floors, the stalls are sectioned off and labeled: cereal, rice, and so on. I see farmers with baskets of potatoes, red and white rice, buckwheat, flour, mushrooms, *lots* of hot chili peppers, a vast assortment of dried cheeses, and freshly slaughtered beef and pork. We come to a collection of dried fish. A pungent odor prickles my nose, making me scrunch up my face. If it were winter, I'm told, I'd see a leg of yak with the hoof still attached. I whisper quiet thanks that it's spring.

The vibrant red, green, and yellow fruits and vegetables are displayed in stacks resembling an endless sky of rainbows. It competes with the traditional clothing made from Bhutanese textiles in a variety of colorful patterns. Weaving between the stalls, I hear the gentle sounds of chanting and the murmur of mantras amid the idle chatter. People here worship everywhere, no matter how public it is. They will stop across the street from a chorten and bow. I can't remember seeing anyone do this back home except for my mother, who taught me to make the sign of the cross whenever I passed a church. I still do it to this day. Chuckling, I have a vision of me suddenly belting out a

Hail Mary or two at the Super Stop & Shop. That would gener-
ate some attention. Passersby would think I was merely suffering
sticker shock in the produce department.

Startled by two teenage girls listening to music, I recognize the
singer and must laugh—Jennifer Lopez has arrived in Bhutan.
Who would have thought?

The women take up residence in front of their stalls. Some
stand, but more often they lie against the huge sacks of rice,
weary from having been here since the crack of dawn. I notice

their worn-out, satchel-like purses on the floor, open and visible
to all who pass, a testament to their lack of attachment to their
limited amount of stuff. That may be another reason they
seem happy and contented with their lives. This level of trust
is foreign to us with our designer purses all zipped up, swung
over shoulders, weighed down with makeup, wallets filled with
money and credit cards, house keys, car keys, medications, and
all manner of other daily must-haves. I think about the other
side of the world where we cling to material things as if they
are our security, our source of happiness. Ultimately the more
stuff we have, the more stuff we want, and the more stuff we're
afraid of losing. A far cry from the Buddhist lifestyle of living

in simplicity. This market scenario is a reminder of the essence of Buddhism, which is a letting go known as nonattachment. It is a way to rid your life of *unnecessary* stuff and a way to become happier. Suddenly Big Red comes to mind. What was I thinking when I packed enough outfits for twenty-two days and almost 500 pills?

At each stall, I am offered samples of food, along with welcoming arms and smiling faces. I do make one purchase when an intoxicating smell reaches my nose. We stop at the booth of the famous Incense Man, who is at the market each weekend selling a variety of organic Bhutanese incense. Because he uses only pure herbs and no added sticks of wood to give it strength, it's considered better than Indian incense.

We come to a covered bridge adorned on all sides with hundreds of prayer flags known as wind horse flags because the wind will spread the prayers and mantras on these flags around the world with the speed of a horse.

Before crossing the bridge, leaning against the archway, Yeshey tells me about *doma*. Made by mixing a betel nut with slaked lime and wrapping it in a betel leaf, doma acts as a mild stimulant, causing a warming sensation in the body and slightly heightened alertness and could be compared to that of drinking a cup of coffee. The effects can vary from person to person.

"See those spots all along the archway and covering the steps leading to the bridge. The red spots are the blood red juice spit by the chewers of doma. The white spots come from the lime powder. You'll see these splattered along almost every village path."

It is as much a part of the culture as the prayer flags. Men and women chew it and it leaves permanent red, clown-like stains on their teeth and mouths. It's also used as a casual offering or gift among friends and strangers. I ask if anyone in Yeshey's family partakes. "No," he says, "because of its harmful effects on the mouth."

I suspect that it might be a contributing factor to the sense of peace and happiness here, but I draw no conclusions.

Having crossed the bridge, we come to the section of the market where carpets, religious items such as prayer wheels, horns and cymbals, bamboo baskets, bowls, textiles, and hats from different ethnic groups are sold. Bargaining is in order if I wish to buy something, but I pass for now. As we leave, I note once more that there isn't an unfriendly face to be found, just lots of red teeth and lips.

Next stop: the National Textile Museum. These luxurious, hand-woven cotton and silk pieces covered with embroidered designs are a distinctly Bhutanese art form. I stand back and

watch the women, called the chief weavers, sitting on the floor with their legs straddling the looms. The looms are fixed vertical frames with pedals and a leather backstrap to support the woman's lower back. The fibers are mainly silk and cotton though the weavers are also known to use yak hair to make more durable items such as tents and coats. With great dexterity, they create their elaborate patterns using multiple sets of yarn. No electricity needed. One young weaver encourages me to look over the goods she has at her side. She releases her hands from the loom and holds up ten fingers. Ten days. That is how long it takes her to make one scarf. It takes a weaver two to three months working ten hours a day just to make a kira. I try to remember not to complain so much about my aching back. She smiles, and I notice that her teeth are not red or rotted, a sign she has refrained from the gift of the doma.

On the ground floor is a gallery displaying a priceless collection of women's and men's garments, scarves, belts, handbags, bed coverlets, sofa covers, book covers, and bookmarks. The museum also houses beautiful Bhutanese clothes from the 1600s to the present. In the small gift shop, I gaze at a gorgeous bedcover priced at $3,000 US. More than any other souvenir, I want to purchase some small pieces of this timeless Bhutanese art form.

Leaving the museum, we pass a group of monks in saffron-colored tank tops playing badminton, while other monks play golf, reaffirming the importance of seeing Bhutan before it becomes too Westernized.

Now we head to the Mothihang Takin Preserve. According to legend, the Divine Madman consumed an entire cow and a goat, then placed the skull of the cow on the body of the goat and created this odd-looking creature, the takin. Originally a mini-zoo, the king felt keeping animals enclosed ran counter to religious and environmental reasons, so the zoo was closed. Because the takins had become domesticated while in captivity, they wandered the busy streets of Thimpu. Safety concerns

made it necessary to keep the takin in an enclosed, forested habitat at the edge of Thimphu, and thus the Takin Preserve was established. I'm not impressed with them, nor they with me. As we walk along the path that circles their fenced-in facility, no amount of cajoling or food can get them to come close to the fence.

As I am sitting in the hotel lobby trying to access the Internet, a nice couple begins to converse with me. They invite me to have dinner with them and I gladly accept. Eating alone is starting to lose its luster. At dinner, I finally eat some solid food, but stay on the American side of the menu just to be safe. The Bhutanese cuisine my new friends are indulging in looks delicious, and I decide to try some. Tomorrow.

As we chat, I ask the opinion of these experienced trekkers on the ingenious solution I've come up with on how to deal with taking a pee or you-know-what in the great outdoors. I tell them that after much thought, my new plan is to pack a large hotel towel in my day bag. I will wrap the towel around my waist, holding it closed with some hair clips, and then squat. I figure that if nature is going to win, I can, at least, make some cover for myself.

"Ellie, don't do that; you'll just get yourself all tangled up in bigger mess. Just do like everyone else, squat and go," Wayne says. Envisioning the possible complications he hints at, I agree and decide it's best to leave the towel hanging on the rack in the hotel bathroom. I sigh and vow to continue to hold out or hold in, whichever comes first.

Getting ready for bed, I reflect on the spectacular places we visited today and the things I've learned about Bhutan and its people, not only from my guide, but from the sights, sounds, and smells that I experienced. It's hard to decide which impression will be the most lasting. Before I turn off the bedside light, I catch a glimpse of Big Red standing empty and waiting, ready to be repacked.

Looking at my stuff spread out all over this tiny room, I realize much of it is unnecessary. My compulsion to drag so much with me is hindering the true spirit and purpose of my journey. I should be more than just an observer of a simpler lifestyle; I should let go of things and make room for what is important. My mantra before I left the States should have been "Be as you see." The logical solution would be to throw caution to the wind, along with most of my clothes, makeup, hair care products, electronics, and the like. I should simply get out of bed tomorrow morning, don my one pair of jeans, throw on my Thai t-shirt, and head out to explore this place where simplicity reigns in abundance.

If we were more in tune with our spiritual nature and cared less about our stuff, we'd have a better hold on our happiness, not to mention our physical health. I can talk the talk but don't always walk the walk. Sighing, I pull up the covers, knowing I'm not yet ready for this.

CHAPTER SIXTEEN

Along the Dochu La Pass

May 11, Meri Puensum Resort, Punakha, Bhutan

After breakfast, we set off on the three-hour ride to Punakha, the former capital of Bhutan. The road climbs rapidly and has the typical twists and turns. I should be used to them by now, but I'm not.

Something else I can't get used to is the sight of poor laborers being dropped off early each morning along the highway and given a spot to clean. I see men strap huge bundles of stone and wood to the backs of women to carry down a steep, muddy path. I watch women, in the rain, sweeping the sides of the road with little makeshift brooms, their small children huddled together under an umbrella for protection. It seems like all they do is sweep dirt from one place to another. They must remain on that assigned section of road until they are picked up at the end of the day or walk miles back home. They do the same job, six days a week, for a pittance a day. This is such a jarring image in a place that is called one of the happiest places on the planet. Something about this just doesn't jive.

We travel through the Dochu La pass. On a clear day there is an incredible view of the snow-capped peaks of the Himalayas including Gangar Punsum—the tallest unclimbed peak in the world. Unfortunately, it is cloudy today. Getting out of the car we can see the forest decorated with thousands of prayer flags strung from tree to tree, fluttering in the wind. The people of Bhutan don't just pray behind closed doors or in temples. Everywhere in this tiny kingdom there is an undeniable and deeply touching sense of freedom in the simplicity of their spirituality in action for the entire world to see. There is something peaceful, healing, and centering about listening to the sound of those flags flapping in the wind. I find myself wanting to stand here, just listening and feeling. No need for brick and mortar. I think about my years feeling stifled or bored by having to sit, kneel, and stand on command—all rote. I couldn't put my finger on it back then, but something is lost in this structured way of praying. That something was my need for a closer spiritual connection to a higher power.

Turning around, we face an immense monument called Druk Wangyal—a huge chorten surrounded by 108 smaller chortens. As a sign of respect, we walk clockwise around the monument before we return to the car.

As the weather begins to clear, we start our long descent into the Punakha and Wangdiphodrong Valleys. The road passes through a forest filled with rhododendrons and magnolias that is followed by orange and banana trees, and finally cactus.

Punakha Valley is famous for the red and white rice that grows along the river valley. Stopping to admire the view, we spot three Buddhist monks bathing in the middle of the river. Is there anything the Bhutanese do not do outdoors?

We take time for lunch at a quaint restaurant. Yeshey joins me, which is a real treat since guides don't usually eat with tourists. We are seated at a large window with a view that overlooks a charming pastoral landscape. The Himalayan mountains make a stunning backdrop for the terraces of lush green rice that stretch as far as the eye can see. It's like a work of art created by man and beast.

In the distance, I spot a large, square mud structure that was once a home occupied by a farmer and his family. The Bhutanese believe that it's unlucky to move into a house once occupied by another family, so the houses are abandoned rather than sold. Some are vacant because of bad karma. Tradition has it that if a family continues to have bad luck under their roof, they must leave it, never to return. The house will remain empty until it crumbles to the ground. I can see a similarity to people back home who walk away from their underwater mortgages and foreclosed homes. I also wonder about my pristine white condo's karma, which seems to get worse with each dog that enters. Perhaps we should just abandon that expensive dwelling of ours and move on, but that thought is quickly discarded!

It's my fourth day in Bhutan, and my appetite continues to improve. For the first time, I'm excited by the prospect of sampling some authentic cuisine. Ever the gentleman, Yeshey orders for me. Red rice and chilies are the primary dishes in this country, and rice finds its way into breakfast, lunch, and dinner. They are passionate about chilies, so passionate that these sacred vegetables are spread out to dry over roadsides, rooftops, and courtyards. They don't add many spices to their food, so their curry is basically chili, and lots of it. They have a saying: If it doesn't make you sweat, then why bother to eat. Another favorite is cheese with chili called *ema datshi*. It is insanely *hot*. I declined that experience. They also dry the datshi over fire and then chew it to keep the body warm. I won't be trying that either.

When it comes to meat, it's all about yak, which is similar to our beef. Not a single part of the animal is wasted. Their milk is made into cheese, and even the skin is fried and served as a snack. I wonder if it is as unappetizing as our beef jerky. Worried about how my stomach will react to my first introduction to Bhutanese cuisine, Yeshey keeps my dish on the lighter side with no meat added.

When our meals arrive, my plate is filled with an assortment of vegetables including fiddleheads, cabbage, potatoes, and red rice, which looks pretty but has no taste. His meal is on the fiery side and includes yak. I'm grateful for his conservative choices for me. Even though my GI tract seems to be on the mend, I don't want to tempt fate.

After lunch, we visit the Punakha Dzong, known as the Palace of Great Bliss. Built in the seventeenth century and made up of twenty-one temples, it is the second oldest and perhaps the most majestic dzong in Bhutan. The surrounding landscape is lovely, with blue mountains on the horizon. It is flanked by the confluence of two prominent rivers, the Pho Chu (Male River) to the right and the Mo Chu (Female River) on the left. A six-story structure, it is adorned with the most ornate, hand-carved, decorative windows and measures 590 feet in length with a width of 236 feet. It has three courtyards and a central tower called an *utse*.

Once inside, it's like being in a time warp. The dzong is the final resting place of some of the country's most revered people. The walls are home to a world of ancient history, culture, and mythology. The extensive collection includes paintings, sculptures, and intricate stone and wooden carvings. I gaze up at the hundreds of beautifully painted dragons that adorn the high ceiling. Also on display is a series of twelve exquisite paintings that depict the birth, life, and death of Buddha. Behind a huge altar are three ten-foot-tall gold-and-silver statues of Buddha, flanked by Guru Rinpoche—who brought Buddhism to Bhutan—and the Zhabdrung, a Tibetan Buddhist lama who unified the country, forming a nation state. It's quiet except for some resident monks chanting in the distance, so I sit and meditate for a while. I feel like pinching myself; I can hardly believe I'm halfway around the world meditating before a sacred statue of Buddha. This feels so outside my realm of books and home-grown attempts

at achieving a sense of Buddhist sacredness. A moving and humbling experience, it brings tears to my eyes. When I rise, I notice that the floor in front of the altar is worn from so many prostrations. There are foot and knee prints deeply embedded in the wood, and in some places an outline of worshippers' heads, a testament to their devotion.

It's been a full day, and my next destination is the Meri Puensum Resort. Situated on a hilltop, it features an outdoor bar that overlooks a spectacular view of the Punakha Valley below—a welcome and calming view after a long day out. The resort is decorated with colorful tiles interspersed with traditional architecture.

Yeshey takes command of Big Red while I check in. He never says a thing about her weight, but I wonder what he thinks each time he strains to pick her up. I know full well what kind of responses I would get in the States. Thankfully I'm only one flight up. My room is clean and tidy but dated. The floors creak and the TV doesn't work. I proceed with my usual routine and unpack Red, once again setting out each item with care. I decide to take a quick shower before I head down to dinner. Fast showers are necessary since the water is not always hot, and the water pressure is usually low.

After a light supper, I take my cup of black tea and sit in the gazebo overlooking the valley. I think about the hotels I stayed in during my years of business travel. I would land at my destination and be met by a driver who would cart my bags to a waiting limousine and whisk me off to an elegant five-star hotel. A bellman would take care of my luggage while I checked into a beautifully appointed suite. If I decided to have in-room dining, I could select from an extensive menu, and my dinner would be brought to my room on a tray decorated with flowers. At the end of my workday, I would luxuriate in the Jacuzzi.

I smile to myself as I take in the view. Such a tranquil location. It's amazing how quiet things are—no traffic, airplanes, TV, or radios. All this silence is a sound. It's called stillness. When I think of it from a spiritual perspective, I realize this is the only time I can quiet the thoughts and chatter in my mind. I am truly in the moment, and all that matters is now. I feel at ease, untroubled by the world or myself, with no need for material possessions or luxuries. *Is this the trade off,* I wonder? If so, I'll take it. Maybe there's hope for me yet.

Back in my room, I update my blog, then do some sketching. I'm trying to design a garment for women who travel to foreign lands with primitive *facilities.* There are some challenges as you can imagine. I drift off to sleep wondering how the coming day's adventure will go. What a precious gift it was to meditate among monks in a Buddhist temple, on Buddhist soil. It reminds me of my first exposure to something called transcendental meditation.

CHAPTER SEVENTEEN

"I believe I can fly."

~R. Kelly

I was introduced to transcendental meditation, aka TM, in 1973. I was watching a talk show featuring His Holiness Maharishi Mahesh Yogi. He was a shrunken little man in a flowing, white robe. He had long, white hair and beard, and sat cross-legged with his sandaled feet on the chair. He professed that practicing TM twice daily could reduce stress, improve your memory, and promote peace and good health. He also stated that he could levitate by meditating. With enough practice, the maharishi said, a person could rise up from the lotus position, move forward, and land. He called this yogic flying.

It reeled me in like a fish on a hook. I could gain the peace of mind I had been searching for, improve my memory, become an enlightened being, and learn how to fly just by sitting quietly for twenty minutes twice a day while silently chanting a single sound.

The two-week TM course cost just twenty-five dollars.

I walked into my first class not knowing quite what to expect, but excited about how this would dramatically change my life. At the time, I was still entrenched in the strict religious dogma of Catholicism. It seemed to be an albatross around my neck, often leaving me confused and disheartened as I tried to navigate through a myriad of challenges. I was convinced TM was my peaceful savior.

There were several rows of people in the small room where we learned how to meditate. After each session we were told to go home and practice for twenty minutes, twice a day. I did this faithfully though I didn't notice any difference in my mind or demeanor, nor did I experience an inch of liftoff. I assumed it would take more practice, especially when it came to yogic flying.

Two weeks later our initiation day arrived. What joy I felt knowing I was going to meet the maharishi in person. I wore a white blouse, long, flowing skirt, and sandals. All I lacked were some flowers in my hair. Our instructors told us to bring a bunch of fresh flowers, a piece of fruit, and a new handkerchief. These items would be our offering to the maharishi. What we would receive in return was a mantra—a sacred sound—specially chosen for each of us.

We were taken one at a time into a room and asked to remove our shoes. Behind closed doors, we would be formally initiated in a private ceremony. You could hear a pin drop as the they escorted me into that tiny room. It was dark save for some candles on a makeshift altar that was covered with a white sheet. It became evident rather quickly that the presence of the maharishi was not in the flesh, but on canvas. Above the altar was a picture of His Holiness. Greatly disappointed, but not wanting to show anything but reverence for him, albeit just a picture, I knelt at the altar. Standing on either side of me, one of the instructors whispered for me to present my offerings. As I stared at the image on the canvas, I remembered being in church and kneeling before the cross. Wasn't that what I was trying to get away from?

The instructors began to sing in Sanskrit—the language of Hinduism and Buddhism. One of them whispered my personal and specially chosen mantra in my ear. I solemnly promised never to say my mantra aloud or to tell it to another living soul. Several minutes later the ceremony was over. On to the next apostle. I was free to go out into the world to find everlasting peace and levitate—maybe even fly—my life forever changed.

I meditated faithfully for several months but became frustrated when I didn't experience any feelings of peace or calm. Not to mention the fact that the closest thing to levitation was my attempts to get off the couch after sitting cross-legged in a full lotus position.

Eventually, life got in the way, and I gave it up for the next twenty-five years. But I never, and I mean never, told anyone, not even Ron, my special mantra. That is, until one summer day when we were at the beach with several of our closest friends. Somehow, we got into a conversation about meditation. To my amazement, my friend's husband had taken the same TM course I had. I can still remember the debate in my head. *Should I tell Joe my mantra if he tells me his? What could possibly happen?* For all I knew, the Maharishi was dead or had levitated to some distant galaxy. I got up the courage. "I'll tell you my mantra if you tell me yours."

And so on that warm, sunny day on a Cape Cod beach, Joe and I shared our well-guarded secret, our personal mantra.

"Shir-ring," I said.

He replied, "Shir-ring."

We stared at each in silence before breaking out in laughter. Perhaps Ron's initial assessment of the whole TM thing was right—a scam.

Were we just gullible Westerners—desperate for a change—who had fallen hook, line, and sinker for a hoax? I read a couple of critical articles several years later. One stated that the maharishi and his disciples were not performing yogic flying. What they were doing was exerting quite a bit of effort as they sat cross-legged to give them the so-called liftoff, followed by a slightly elevated movement forward, and then landing with a thud. The other article said a US district court jury awarded a man $137,890 in a case against two transcendental meditation organizations that falsely promised he could learn to fly. He claimed that he had suffered psychological and emotional damage during his eleven-year association with TM. Now, why hadn't I thought of that?

Twenty-five years, two children, several careers, and no meditating later, I was still struggling to find some relief from stress and a deeper meaning in my life. It's not that I was unhappy, but I had a growing sense of discontent and incompleteness. I felt rudderless, without a real sense of purpose, whatever that meant.

During the summer of 1999, some life-altering challenges plunged me into the depths of depression. I ventured into a bookstore adjacent to a yoga studio and was drawn to the book *Wherever You Go, There You Are*, written by a contemporary Western Buddhist, Jon Kabat-Zinn. It brought me back to meditation from an entirely different perspective. My new take on meditation started a journey of introspection and self-discovery. I found myself becoming more aware of my need for perfection as well as more *stuff*. But despite hours spent in meditation, it slowly became apparent that I needed one hell of a wake-up call. It would turn out to be a journey halfway around the world with a most unlikely teacher: *Big Red*.

CHAPTER EIGHTEEN

Butter tea, cell phones, and Hello Kitty

May 12, Punakha/Wangdue Phodrang, Bhutan

We are hiking through a patchwork quilt of brown and green rice paddies. There are small clusters of houses with nearby chortens, many containing sacred relics. As we head toward a hamlet of several farmers' homes, I see two people in the distance stop to share a quid of doma. It's so different back home. How many of us spot someone we know then quickly do an about-face and head in the opposite direction simply because we're too busy to stop and chat?

The farmhouses are a mixture of Tibetan and Chinese architecture, colorfully painted with special designs and symbols. Large and squarish, they are constructed of mud, bamboo, and wood, and can withstand harsh elements. The roofs are wooden shingles held down by stones. Three stories high, the ground floor houses cattle and other livestock. The second floor is for storage, and the third floor is the living quarters. The open area between the third floor and the roof is used to dry hay, vegetables, meats, and red chilies. The most important feature is the prayer flag in the center of the roof, erected to protect the house and its family.

Because I'm not traveling with a group, we are graciously invited in for a visit. It doesn't matter that the farmer has been out in the fields or that his family is busy with household chores. Everything comes to a halt so that they can welcome us into their home. It's the kind of hospitality many Westerners have forgotten in the hustle and bustle of our busy lives. The farmer leads the way as we pass cows and goats. We follow him up a ladder with steps made from tree trunks. Their third floor living space is divided into a small kitchen, a main room used as a bedroom, a bathroom, and a room for their household altar. The altar is colorfully painted and decorated with photographs, flowers, beads, rice, cakes, and other symbolic items. It's adorned with a statue of the Guru Rinpoche, the Buddha, and others I don't recognize. Small butter lamps are always lit, and water—symbolizing purity and humility—is offered daily. Just as in the temples, the floorboards have imprints from hundreds of prostrations. The elders in the household often do as many as a thousand of these each day. The family sits on the floor to eat and sleeps there on blankets. This family is lucky; they not only have a stove, but they are one of the few who have a TV. The home is so bare, yet there on the kitchen counter is a TV.

We proceed to the main room where the farmer sets out bowls of flattened maize, toasted rice, and a large silver pot of hot butter tea that rests on a yellow straw basket. His face is weathered and wrinkled. Dirt and dried blue paint are embedded in his fingernails and the cracks of his hands. It's a delight to be here sharing tea with them.

Where we just buy a box of tea bags and dunk, in this country making tea is quite a process. The tea leaves are first boiled in water for half a day until the liquid gets dark brown. After being

skimmed, it is shaken several times in a large cylinder with some fresh yak butter and salt.

When drinking butter tea, you take a sip, and the host refills your cup to the brim. A visitor never drains his cup but allows the host to top it off. Etiquette is always observed so the host will not be offended. If the visitor does not wish to drink a lot, the best thing to do is to leave the tea untouched and then drink it just before you depart. There is also a tea tradition in which you dip your ring finger into the cup and then flick the liquid up in the air three times before you drink. This is considered a blessing. It's exciting for me to be able to participate in their daily rituals while learning more about the Bhutanese culture.

My mouth is watering as I wait for the butter tea. I am ready for some warmth and comfort. The farmer gives me a toothless grin as he ladles tea into a white, plastic teacup decorated with tiny flowers. I take the cup, expecting a subtle but welcome taste. After several tentative sips, I know they will be my last. The butter makes the tea very rich, very heavy, with a highly unpleasant taste, and it's barely warm. Ugh, I try not to make a face. As I put my cup down the farmer immediately tops it off. I don't want to insult him or his family, but it will be a bigger insult if I drink it and proceed to vomit. Watching me closely, Yeshey leans toward me and says, "Don't worry. It's fine if you don't drink any more." Relieved, I smile a thank-you.

The farmer's wife and their two little girls join us. She entertains one of them by painting her toenails with bright-purple polish. It's touching to watch. We are worlds apart, but we are both mothers. The farmer waves a white cloth over our teacups. I think this is a blessing but soon realize he is shooing the flies buzzing around us. The ornate carved panels that cover the windows are wide-open so it's an easy entry for all flying

insects. Add that to the Buddhist belief of doing no harm to all things breathing, and well... With the collection of flies lingering on top of the parched rice and maize, I pretend to eat the tiny amount I've taken into my hands while discretely dropping pieces behind me.

I look around this modest—primitive by Western standards—farm dwelling. The dark-blue-painted walls are cracked and peeling. The planked floor is rough and stained. The only furnishings are the bright-red decorative rugs that are threadbare and worn. I ask myself, *Does this define happiness? Or is happiness achieved despite this simple existence? Had I romanticized what I expected to see and experience during all those months of planning?*

An image of my condo pops into my head. The kitchen with every appliance known to man, and the immaculate counters and floor. Everything in my home is washed and sanitized to the nth degree. My well-stocked fridge and white cabinets full of carefully stored food are a testimony to comfort and security. I have everything a woman could want. No fly would dare knock on my door. How ironic that I'm thousands of miles from home and seeking a glimpse of happiness. What's wrong with this picture?

While Yeshey converses with the farmer, I wonder again about the impact that Westernization will have on this tiny kingdom. I'm brought back to reality when Yeshey—accustomed to my bathroom issues—decides to show me a traditional farmhouse toilet. We've developed a relatively close bond in the short time we've spent together. Kiddingly, he has begun to call me his Bhutanese son. He leads me to a balcony. At the back of the balcony is a little partition, behind which I get a close-up view of the pit hole. Bewildered, I look at him. "Where does the waste go?" not sure I want to know the answer. He points down. "They are called long-drop toilets." I gawk. Apparently, the crap drops three stories to the ground. *Jesus,* I think, *how much worse can this get?* Then I see a pile of flat sticks that look like tongue depressors lying next to the infamous pit. I'm hoping they're kindling. Nope. "Ouch," I mouth silently. With no toilet paper, I guess they must improvise. "How in the world do they use these?"

He replies with a slight smile, "East to West."

I guess that makes sense to me, but wouldn't a handful of leaves be a softer choice? I wonder, do they give a heads-up before they drop their load—like yelling *duck* or *run? Oy gevalt* is all I can think. It's Yiddish—look it up.

On our way out we pass several family members—grandma included—sitting on the floor, huddled around a huge bag of betel nuts. Looking up, they offer me their biggest, brightest red-stained smiles while crushing the nuts with a wooden tube. Packing them neatly away in burlap bags, they look like a family of squirrels getting ready for a long winter. I had seen ready-made bags of the nut in the markets but was told that real betel lovers make their own. As we're leaving, Yeshey comments that a meal or a snack often ends with the passing around of betel nuts to all, guests included. Trust me, I'm not the least bit disappointed when they don't offer me one.

Glancing back at this family gathering of young and old reinforces my impression that Bhutanese families take care of one another. Respect for and obedience to their elders are the core of the family code of ethics. How different from the US, where our elderly are often neglected and left to live out their lives in sterile, uncaring environments. These kind, compassionate people, who have so little, yet give so much, embody the family values that

Americans talk about but rarely practice.

Walking toward the fields, we observe women bottle-feeding their livestock and washing clothes in pans outside. Even if the farmhouse is near the side of the road, many continue with their daily hygiene outside.

We approach a stone hut and we go inside. No need to ask permission. A woman, barefoot and dressed in a kira, sits on a slab of wood in front of a fire pit stirring rice in a heavy metal pan. Large baskets of uncooked rice surround her. It's cool inside except for the

heat of the fire. The floor is made of dirt, and ashes are everywhere. She greets me with a wide grin and offers me a seat next to her. For obvious reasons I decide not to sit. Instead I crouch next to her. Yeshey gets ready to take our picture. She leans into me and I put my arm around her shoulder. My grin stretches across my face. It feels like family. Before we leave I bow to her, my hands folded in prayer position as I say, "Namaste." Her eyes crinkle when she smiles. No communication barrier. This she understands.

Near one farmhouse we come upon a large rectangular, water-filled wood basin with giant metal tongs leaning against it. Divided into two sections, one is smaller than the other. Next to the basin is a pile of stones sitting on top of a stack of firewood. The stones are heated in a fire, then transferred to the smaller section of the basin with the tongs. The stones heat the water, and as many as three people can sit in the larger section. This is the Bhutanese version of a hot tub. Yeshey says he has one, and it's wonderful. People pay thousands of dollars for fancy hot tubs like this crude, but effective version.

As we near our car, we spot a little boy playing with a stick stuck in an old shoe. He runs in circles giggling and laughing while pushing the shoe around in the dirt. It reminds me of a simpler time when kids would open their gifts and then play with the boxes they came in. Despite painted fingernails and toes, simplicity still reigns in the happiest place on Earth.

When we stop at a resort for lunch, I notice a lot of sheets hanging on lines. Curious, I'm told that this is how some of the hotels wash their guests' linens. Bhutan's pit toilets and hand-washed sheets are now stacked against some of my favorite comforts back home.

Our next stop is Wangdu, the last town before you reach central Bhutan. It's small but has a bustling market. As we stroll along, something red, white, and pink catches my eye, something I never dreamed I'd see in Bhutan: a Hello Kitty tote bag vying for attention against a backdrop of vegetables, baskets loaded with

red and white rice, bushels of incense, burlap bags of peanuts and betel nuts. It's such a dichotomy seeing the Bhutanese people in their native dress with little girls in colorful, lacy dresses and pink plastic shoes; men in jeans; and monks, young and old, leaning against huge prayer wheels while talking on cell phones. In one temple, a group of nuns comes in to pray after leaving their Adidas backpacks and Nike sneakers outside the door.

My itinerary includes a visit to a local school here. Approaching the entrance, I see kids in native attire laughing and talking as they change classes. In the hallway, I snap a photo of one of the many quotes posted on the wall: "Doing good to others is not a duty. It is a joy, for it increases your own health and happiness." The laughter, the uniforms, the jostling and running up the stairs to get to class are all very Western. The quote, not so much!

Classes are taught in English, so I sit in on a math class where the students are learning about decimals. It is interesting how well-behaved and studious the children are compared to the young monks I'd seen attending school inside the temple. They had been sitting in small groups, supposedly studying. Of the thirty or so, just a handful had appeared to be doing anything resembling schoolwork. The rest had been fooling around, laughing, and eating a load of candy or throwing it at one another. It is difficult for me to comprehend; compared to them, the public school children appear better behaved and more orderly in the classroom. It seems that somehow, after spending nine years in a temple, they grow up to become well-disciplined monks, for the most part. Yeshey confided that the teenage monks sneak out after hours, put on their jeans and Nike sneakers, and go to discos to drink and party. The craziest part is that they can't hide the fact that they are monks—their shaved heads are a dead giveaway. Then they sneak back into the monastery before the doors are locked. If they get caught or don't make it back in time, they are punished in front of their peers. This whole scenario sounds just like teenagers back home. I guess no matter where you grow up, there's no escaping punishment for not following the rules.

I am back at my hotel sitting alone under the gazebo, my standard cup of black tea in hand. Night is falling, and the red rays of the setting sun light up the sky above the Punakha Valley. The only sounds are the chirping birds rustling in the trees. I'm tired but content, reflecting on the highlights of the last two days. Words cannot describe the spell-binding beauty of the Docha La pass, where thousands of prayer flags were waved in the deep chasm between two mountain ridges dotted with temples and houses. As the wind passed over the surface of the flags, I breathed in the blessings, good will, and compassion they offered. It was gratifying to know they are there to create happiness for everyone, no matter your religion, color, or position in life. Such a simple way to honor and respect the entirety of life. Perhaps it's something we should consider here. One flag would be sufficient to send the message, but we would probably drive by it and never notice. It's a cultural thing here, born from thousands of years of tradition and deep reverence.

The intense visceral feeling of meditating in front of a ten-foot, golden Buddha will stay with me forever while the sight of Hello Kitty competing for space next to burlap bags of betel nuts will make me laugh. There was the time spent with the farmer and his family, participating and observing their austere lifestyle and the labor-intensive job of planting, tilling, and harvesting crops. The young girl outside washing clothes in a basin, the old woman seated on a piece of wood stirring rice over a fire for hours in a simple stone hut with a dirt floor. No one had a frown on their face. Like the prayer flags that brave the weather, the people of Bhutan brave life. All they need is their family and the land they live on to keep them happy, at least for now. So uncomplicated, so basic. Unlike us, they seek contentment and happiness inside themselves.

I suddenly have a mental image of being back home in my all-white, 3,000-square-foot condo, telling my husband we need to move to a smaller place. One where you spread your arms and can touch the walls. I tell him, "Ron let's plant a garden and live off the land. Let's simplify, get rid of…" I shake my head. *What a ludicrous idea, Ellie.* I get up, stretch, and yawn. Another busy day tomorrow. I enter my room and look around. I see the clothes, makeup, Waterpik, and curling iron. This is my lifestyle. But it's all transitory, easily gone, missing or lost. I traveled several days with just the clothes on my back. I arrived in Bhutan reeking of vomit and looking like something the cat dragged in. Yet I survived, no worse for the wear. I walk over to Big Red. She's empty. I get it. But it's not as simple as ridding myself of my possessions. It's the attachment to my stuff and how it impacts my life—a source of security, gratification, and comfort. How easy it is to get hooked. How difficult to let go.

CHAPTER NINETEEN

Phallic decor, anyone?

May 12, Chime Lhakhang Temple, Thimpu, Bhutan

Besides playing a part in the birth of the tarkin, the Divine Mad Monk, Drukpa Kunley, was well-known for destroying demons. According to Bhutanese historians, he shot an arrow from Tibet and said that wherever it landed a monastery would appear. As he searched for his arrow, he caroused across the countryside, slaying demons and granting *enlightenment* to all the young women with whom he came in contact, using the mystical powers of his *flaming thunderbolt*. Enlightenment in this case is a far cry from the definition with which I'm familiar. Here it means sex, sex, and more sex. Known as the saint of 5,000 women, the Mad Monk's sexual imagery is everywhere in Bhutan. It reflects the belief that carnal relations are a gateway to enlightenment. Anyone want the name of an excellent travel agent?

Apparently the Divine Mad Monk's flaming thunderbolt is not a symbol for bad weather. He is so adored that this conservative society that never shows affection in public is really into his thunderbolt. They protect their homes, stores, and hotels from evil spirits and promote fertility by painting the monk's thunderbolt on their walls, often encircled by a colorful bow. It also protects against quarrels between family members. Hmm, this might be useful to have back home.

As we drive past a restaurant, I catch a glimpse of two divine thunderbolts painted on its facade. Shocked and totally unprepared, I shake my head. I need to get a better look at what must have been my eyes playing tricks. "Dawa, can you please back up?" The car pulls up alongside the white-washed restaurant. Nope, no trick. The length, diameter, and overall stature of these thunderbolts takes my breath away. There is an image of two ten-foot-long penises facing each other and spitting out a stream of *something*. No time to wonder what that *something* is, because all I can focus on is their size. I am dumbstruck.

And it doesn't end there. The Divine Mad Monk's flaming thunder-

bolt comes in various sizes and color schemes, and has a variety of embellishments. Some have eyes while others feature hairy, *ahem*, balls. Of course, all are fully erect. Anything that can be is made into penis shapes: walking sticks, key chains, and a wide variety of trinkets. Clusters of wooden phalluses dangle from rooftops, resembling pornographic wind chimes. In concert with the fluttering prayer flags, you can see, and hear, the tinkling of flying johnsons everywhere. I wonder if our condo association would approve of me hanging one outside our front door? I might just get approval once I explain that it's solely for protection from evil spirits. Perhaps it will work on incontinent dogs?

On the same general train of thought, our next stop is the Chime Lhakhang Temple, one of the most visited and significant destinations for women seeking fertility blessings. Nature's beauty greets us as we walk toward the temple perched on a hillside in the middle of some rice fields. Following several native women, we pass rows of terraced fields, an occasional lonely haystack, and one little boy with an enormous bundle of hay on his back. Just outside the temple are several monks hanging their saffron-colored robes to dry on a line tied between two trees. Next to them are several families taking advantage of the warm, sunny day to picnic on the grass. They invite several stray dogs to join them in their feast.

Baby monks-in-training—boys as young as six—are everywhere. Curious and friendly, they love posing for pictures. Once inside the temple I watch as a monk blesses the women, first gesturing toward them with a bow and arrow, and then holding a large, wooden penis over their heads. These blessings represent the power of the Divine Mad Monk to assist women in getting pregnant. Although the room hums with flies, noise, and tourists, it is also full of an unmistakable feeling of hopefulness. Although I'm way past child-bearing age, I get in line for the blessing—I can't pass up this experience. It is certainly more personal than being incensed in a church full of people.

There is a plethora of penises at every turn. It's fair to wonder at this point how a once devote Catholic girl could end up happily being blessed with a wooden penis held over her head. What will be next on my spiritual journey?

CHAPTER TWENTY

So why Buddhism?

"The first step toward getting somewhere is to decide
that you are not going to stay where you are."
~John Pierpont Morgan

I was eighteen when I met my first husband. At twenty-one, I married him with all the fanfare of a big wedding. Less than a year later I was heading for divorce court despite being told by an unsympathetic priest that I would be excommunicated by the Church if I ever chose to marry again.

My life at that point was a series of losses beginning with the discovery of a cheating husband in a motel room and the devastating loss of my faith and connection to the Church—the one place that had given me comfort and strength since childhood.

Not only had my husband stolen my innocence, but he'd completely stripped our apartment of every stick of furniture, every lamp, every curtain. He didn't stop there. He wiped out our bank account, which included our wedding gifts and savings bonds. Sadly, much of the account had been established with my personal savings built up before our marriage. Realizing that I no longer had a nickel to my name, humiliation was quickly replaced with an anger I didn't think was possible. I was officially pissed off. It was short-lived as I tried to navigate my life in a world of hurt, grief, embarrassment, and shame in the months until the divorce was final.

As I waited for the days and weeks to pass, my life slowly began to take a new direction; my mind was no longer held hostage by grief and sorrow. Smiling, and even laughing, replaced my tears. In the subtlest of ways, my heart began to soften, and I started to let go of what could have been, of what should have been and now wasn't. I'm not sure what gave me the strength to keep moving forward other than a relentless determination not to let this mess get the best of me.

When the court date arrived, I stood alone and took my turn in front of the judge. Before I could take a breath, the divorce degree was granted. Leaving the courthouse, I felt a lightness and sense of freedom that I'd been missing for a long time. Walking toward my car, I abruptly stopped in the middle of the courtyard. With people milling around me and traffic going by, and with no forethought, I took off my platinum wedding band, stretched out my arm, and threw that ring as far and high as I could. Like a rag on a blackboard, I erased my husband's persona from my life. But some things are not so easily undone, even with time—such as the control the Catholic Church continued to have over me.

Several years after the divorce, after I'd remarried and had a child, I was still immersed in all things Catholic but found myself becoming resentful. I didn't want to be branded a divorcée for the rest of my life, like a woman wearing a scarlet letter, or have to live with the fact that I could still attend Mass but was not allowed to participate fully in the sacraments. This had to change.

Three years into my marriage to my second husband, Ron, I began the process of a formal annulment of my first marriage. The Church required that my former spouse be notified. Although I hadn't spoken to him in more than six years, I tracked him down. I wrote him, asking for his support in the annulment process. After receiving his letter of agreement,

I forwarded the documentation to the Tribunal Office of the diocese for them to decide whether my marriage was invalid according to church law. In a matter of weeks, my marriage was annulled. I was now officially reinstated in the Catholic Church.

Almost twenty years later I discovered that I no longer felt that strong connection and closeness to God in church. Something else was brewing inside me. Despite the annulment, I realized I'd never let go of the bitterness that I felt about the Church's laws regarding divorce and remarriage. I had held on to the anger that as a trusting twenty-two-year-old, completely devoted to her religion and married less than a year with no children, I was punished for the sins of her spouse. I never forgot the humiliation of going through that divorce, despite it being the only intelligent choice I had.

Releasing myself from the Church and realizing that I no longer needed it, I began to take note of the feelings of unworthiness and guilt that had plagued me since childhood. Around the age of fifty, I realized that I didn't want to live a life filled with sin and repentance. I needed a new truth that would feed my soul, but I didn't know how to go about finding it. My daughter's gift of a book written by the Dalai Lama was my introduction to Buddhism. More books followed, and I developed a fascination with Buddhist beliefs. It wasn't long before its teachings guided me to a different kind of spiritual path.

Buddhism offers me a wellspring of tools including meditation, yoga, and self-reflection as I seek to free myself from confusion and negativity. These practices allow me to consider alternative ways of responding to life, such as becoming still, and tuning in to the inner wisdom of my being, while cultivating the voice of reason and self-love. Despite all this, when it comes to prayer, God is who I turn to, not Buddha. I don't believe either one makes you closer to the Divine.

Although I'm not a graduate, I consider myself an honorary one because I find the Buddhist teachings and philosophy at the center of my self-discovery and spiritual journey. Buddhism offers me the possibility of living a simpler, more authentic lifestyle. None of this comes naturally to me, even as I seek to experience and better understand Buddhist values throughout my *trip of a lifetime*.

CHAPTER TWENTY-ONE

Leaving the "happy place"

May 12, Silver Pine Hotel, Paro, Bhutan

Back at the hotel on my last evening in Bhutan, I am getting ready for a farewell dinner with Yeshey, and Dawa. Before coming to Asia I was told that giving gifts is more important here than it is in the West. I find that hard to believe. Perhaps if the word *important* were replaced with *appreciated*, it would make more sense to me. And boy did I bring gifts. Did I mention that I had packed, along with everything else, a dozen or more bright yellow-and-blue Western New England College t-shirts and some Soccer Academy t-shirts from my husband, Ron's, camp? Now I'm a little hesitant about giving the t-shirts because I don't want my new friends to think they're not an appropriate gift. But after having to lift Big Red a few times myself, appropriate or not, I'm unloading them. This should lighten Big Red enough that I won't have to let go of any must-haves.

They are thrilled with the shirts, so I ask them to put them on for a picture of the three of us. They joyfully, and I mean joyfully, comply. Dawa keeps touching his chest, saying he feels like sunshine. I will miss them both very much. They have taken such good care of me. I will venture to say that this is typical of the Bhutanese. I have not seen a single angry face or heard an impatient voice—just a lot of smiles and obvious lightheartedness. In fact, in one hotel lobby, an American male was loudly expressing his displeasure about something to one of the hotel staff. The young Bhutanese boy responded with the utmost grace, never appearing distressed or defensive. This has got to be in their DNA. I hope my future guides will be able to match the natural attentiveness and kindness of the ones I have been blessed with here in Bhutan.

May 13, Paro airport, Bhutan, early morning.

As I wait to depart for Nepal, I have time to reflect on my stay here. I am so glad I came. For now, this tiny mountain kingdom has preserved its identity and natural beauty, mystical religion, vibrant culture, and charming people despite having stepped out of their self-imposed isolation and into the modern world of television, cell phones, and the Internet.

Can they continue to preserve their traditional values and remain one of the last unspoiled frontiers? One can imagine that this remote kingdom will have to work hard to protect itself from the ongoing infiltration of technology, pop music, pink plastic shoes, Hello Kitty, Nike sneakers, Adidas backpacks, and contemporary dress. Jigme Khesar Namgyel Wangchuck, Bhutan's current king, claims to have great confidence in his people's understanding of what is right. He feels that it is possible to maintain a happy balance between their traditions and new cultural developments. The Bhutanese appear to be thriving with this new way of living.

The symbols of Bhutan's religion, displayed throughout the country, leave me with unforgettable impressions: the chortens dotting the landscape; the little stupas tucked into crevices along the mountain ridges that honor the dearly departed; the colorful, wind-frayed prayer flags; the endless mountaintop monasteries and riverside dzongs; and of course, the phallic images. Buddhism is everywhere, shaping attitudes and molding thoughts. From the high lamas to the ever-faithful farmers, their deep, abiding faith permeates every aspect of life. It is more than a religion. It is the air they breathe. These are people fully aware of their moral and spiritual influences. Even the maroon-robed monks golfing on the one-and-only golf course ask all who play to circle and apologize to a tree if their ball hits it. So unlike our throwing of clubs and kicking of bags, not to mention the litany of profanities. Can you imagine an American golfer apologizing to a tree?

It is hard for me to wrap my mind around the idea that this culture is guided by the concept of Gross National Happiness, especially after seeing the day-to-day reality of hard labor: working in the fields, caring for livestock, sweeping streets, building shrines, etc.—none of which is mechanized. Departing, I'm left with two questions: Do the people of Bhutan believe they are living in Shangri-La? And if this is truly one of the happiest places on Earth, what is their secret?

I can say with certainty that, despite the meekest of lifestyles or maybe because of it, what the Bhutanese lack in material wealth, they make up for with their never-ending generosity and graciousness. With their endearing smiles and soft-spoken words, they exude a purity of heart and spirit that knows no boundaries. They manifest the most salient characteristics of Buddhism: loving kindness to all sentient beings. Flying over

Paro for the last time, my lasting memory will be of the farmer's faith in a different kind of wireless communication, the prayer flags sending their message: "Each time the wind blows it takes our prayers straight to heaven. No machines or electronics required." Will Nepal be another land of peace and contentment? If so, then I will have some serious food for thought to take home with me.

On a lighter note, I pat myself on the back. I made it through Bhutan squat-free and proud of it! However, Big Red continues to prove herself as heavy as ever, despite unloading those t-shirts. I have already navigated six airports, and not one of them has been easy. Have I learned anything about attachment—or better yet, nonattachment? Will this journey be a test of my stubbornness and endurance or of finding a path to personal enlightenment?

Months after returning home, I will still remember how the people of Bhutan struggle with so little to show for it. I will finally hit on the answer to the question: Why is Bhutan considered the happiest place on Earth? In the West, we have a built-in greed gene, or *more* factor. Our attachment and craving for more stuff is exacerbated by a culture that favors the notion that we will never have enough to make us happy. This path of more is the cause of our greatest suffering. In Bhutan, it's not about more. Some might think the Bhutanese are other-worldly, but human nature is the same no matter who you are or where you live. The difference is in how we live our lives. It seems that in the land of happiness, the inner mind-set is all about being content with what you have.

CHAPTER TWENTY-TWO

Welcome to Nepal, Ellie and Big Red

May 13, Kathmandu, Nepal

The kingdom of Nepal is situated between China and India. As I fly in from Paro, I'm welcomed by the breathtaking snowy peaks of the Himalayas and Annapurnas. Everyone should have the chance to experience this spectacular view at least once. From the first time I saw a photograph of these peaks, I've had a deep longing to witness their majestic glory. So deeply rooted into the earth's core, they stand strong and fearless against the winds of time and nature. There is something quite spiritual about them. I never imagined I would be having such a close encounter with them.

Nepal's capital, Kathmandu, lies in the Valley of the Gods, and our descent is dramatic. As on my flight into Paro, it seems as if we are flying straight into the mountains when suddenly the sky opens up, and we swoop over rooftops before finally touching down. I'm grateful that the barf bag stays neatly tucked into the seat pocket this time.

After wrestling Big Red off the baggage carousel, I perform a balancing act similar to the one at JFK, but this time without a push cart. I'm unable to move more than a few feet before my carry-on slides off my shoulder, followed by my laptop and duffel bag, and finally Big Red careens to the floor with a thud. The walk, or should I say crawl, to the exit is torturous. What should take minutes, stretches into more than an hour. I can only imagine what I look like to the people whizzing by, to say nothing of the unlucky travelers who stumble over me as I try to collect all my stuff. Avoiding eye contact, I overhear comments that are definitely not Buddha-like.

I'm worried that my driver will leave because it has taken so long to reach the exit, and my gaze bounces around the sea of travelers and signs. On the verge of losing it, I turn and spot: WELCOME ELLIE DIAS. The tour operator greets me warmly, then struggles to lift Big Red and place her in his car trunk. His upturned smile has turned into a downward frown. "Awfully heavy," he says with forced patience. "You are only staying a few days?" A flush creeps across my cheeks. I nod. With that "way too heavy" mantra in my head, I see the handwriting on the wall again: Big Red is more than anyone can handle.

I am totally unprepared for what I see as we drive through Kathmandu. It looks like a city rushing into the modern era with concrete buildings on the rise. And the driving? There is no rhyme or reason to it; it can only be described as all over the place. It doesn't seem to matter that the roads have two lanes. Almost every vehicle looks ready for the trash heap; clearly there are no auto body shops here. Gaudy, honking rickshaws and scooters weave in and out of the traffic, every vehicle jockeying for space. The sights, sounds, and smells leave me with sensory overload—a real shocker after quiet, serene Bhutan.

Almost everyone is wearing a mask over their nose and mouth. Fidgeting, I ask the driver if there's an outbreak of the swine flu.

"No," he says, "if you want to breathe here you need to wear a mask to filter out the dirt and dust in the air."

Relieved, I notice the dirt isn't keeping women from wearing their beautiful, silk saris as they ride sidesaddle on motorbikes. Against the colorful blur are mounds of garbage lining the street. I get a powerful whiff of an odor I would have preferred not to encounter.

Children tucked between their parents or perched on handlebars whizz by on motorbikes. Their balancing act seems outdone only by the piles of stuff people are carrying on their heads. Men of all ages, in various garb, walk with their ducks or goats and wrestle with the occasional cow that chooses to sleep on the road. Altogether it's a wild welcome. Curious how Nepal is going to stack up against Bhutan in the happiness department, I soon have an answer. My smile vanishes when I notice children sleeping on the pavement and pedestrian crossings. Groups of them dig through the trash while others beg on street corners. Tears sting my eyes. "Is there no one to care for these children?"

"They are street children; over 5,000 of them live in the cities of Nepal. Many are victims of abuse, runaways. They live off scraps of food they find, and many sniff glue to forget their hunger," he said, his voice catching.

What must it be like to witness this sight every day? Their grim little faces watch, forlorn and abandoned, buried beneath pain and isolation. One can find homeless children anywhere, and I know Bhutan has its fair share, but it seems contradictory in a place where contentment and peace are said to reign. The first noble truth of Buddhism states that it is impossible to live without experiencing suffering, but when it involves children, it is difficult to accept.

"So it seems suffering is universal. It's the one thing Buddhists, Christians and Muslims are all worried about."
~ John Greene

CHAPTER TWENTY-THREE

David Beckham and Snickers bar momos

May 13, Niti's place, Kathmandu, Nepal

I will be staying with Niti, the sister of Asian Pacific Adventures' owner. This will be my home base as I tour Nepal, and travel to and from the jungle and Tibet.

We turn off the main drag and down several filthy, narrow streets. I miss the lush greenery of Bhutan. I grin. I doubt that cannabis will be poking through the sidewalks here. Despite the tight quarters, vehicles pass within inches of each other, accompanied by nonstop honking and yelling. Driving in Nepal calls for commando-like survival skills. We approach a pair of huge, solid gates where a guard checks the driver's credentials and looks inside the car to do a passenger check. Satisfied, he opens the gates, and we enter a stunning courtyard with tables, benches, and a huge fountain surrounded by a garden bursting with flowers. To the right of the garden is a restaurant that my host owns.

A quiet young man, Ram Hari, approaches and bows, his hands folded in prayer position over his heart, and says, "*Namaste.*"

Bowing, I return the greeting. The ground floor of Niti's home serves as a school: Career Building for Women. Ram attempts to carry Big Red as he leads the way up the two flights of stairs to my room. He is the first person who actually smiled when picking up Big Red—that is, before he began to move it. This is true

Buddhism in action: loving kindness for one and all, including Big Red. I decline when he offers to help me unpack. Enough strange men have already helped with my personal items on this trip. A few moments later, he returns to bring me to a sitting area to meet my hostess. Passing room after room, each impeccably decorated with religious objects and beautiful artwork, I can hardly contain my excitement over staying in a villa in Nepal with all the comforts of home.

Dressed in an elegant, silk sari, Niti is a delightful, charming woman. After the initial introductions, she explains what I can expect during my stay. She insists that I treat this as if it were my home, and she means it. She has ordered a light lunch for me at her restaurant, and this evening we will dine together.

My room, which belongs to one of her sons, is bright and spacious, but hanging over the bed—where one would expect a picture religious in nature—is a huge poster of David Beckham. I suppose this might be appropriate since he *is* considered a god in the soccer world. So it is here, under the watchful eyes of David Beckham, that I will fall asleep wondering, *Where the hell is Buddha?*

I open the door to find my way through the maze of hallways to the ground floor, and then the restaurant for lunch. Standing outside my room is Ram Hari, ready and waiting for me. This is how it will be for my entire stay. He will be at my beck and call, walking me to and from the restaurant, the gardens, downtown, anywhere I want to go, and will bring me anything I need. Another young man on Niti's staff provides me with plenty of water, tea, and coffee. He turns down my bed at night and leaves cookies at my bedside. Completely unexpected. No hotel back home can compare.

At the restaurant, I lunched on *momos*, a type of dumpling native to the Himalayan region of Tibet. Similar to Chinese dumplings, these are filled with all sorts of meats, cheeses, and vegetables, and can be steamed or fried. Quite popular with foreigners are the sweet momos, filled with Mars or Snickers candy bars. With David Beckham in my bedroom and Snickers momos, *where am I?*

Overcome by exhaustion, I beg off the afternoon touring. I return to my David Beckham sanctuary and get some much-needed rest. For the first time in days, I have the opportunity to lie down, light some incense, and meditate before dinner.

The top floor of the home is Niti's dining room, complete with a personal chef. We dine with another guest named Chris. He has stayed here before during his travels in Nepal and Tibet. It's a welcome change from eating alone.

We are served a spiced meat with a rice dish that is popular in Nepal. The food is delicious, and thankfully, black tea is served.

Later, drifting off to sleep, relieved to be where the amenities are more familiar, I wonder whether Nepal is embracing Western ways at a faster pace than Bhutan? Perhaps when I visit some villages tomorrow, it will become clearer.

CHAPTER TWENTY-FOUR

Lights out!

May 14, Niti's place, Kathmandu, Nepal

My alarm clock buzzes at 6 A.M. In keeping with my routine, I rise two hours early to get ready for my day's adventures. Normally, I start with my morning readings, followed by some quiet meditation. I then move on to plugging in the curling iron as well as the iron to press my outfit for the day. This is followed by a meticulous application of makeup.

But today is different. After turning off the alarm, I try to turn on the bedside lamp. Nothing, no light. I get up and flick the switch for the overhead light. Nothing. I precariously navigate my way to the bathroom, fumble for the switch. Again, nothing.

I have no idea how I will accomplish my morning routine before breakfast. Remembering the flashlight by my bedside, I attempt to apply my makeup with one hand while using the other to aim the flashlight at the bathroom mirror. Not an easy task.

Shining it on my clothes, I try to smooth out my wrinkled sundress. Staring at my cold, lifeless curling iron, I grimace, realizing my only choice is to cover what will be a bad hair day with a hat. This is just another reminder of my need to maintain an aura of being perfectly dressed, made up, and coiffed during this trip, forgetting that the people here are too busy living their lives to care how I look.

Just as I'm about to head out, my room lights up like a Christmas tree. I glance back at my abandoned appliances lying on top of Big Red. Is there a message here?

At least I know now why I was told to bring a flashlight on this trip—advice I had ignored of course. In Kathmandu—population 700,000—much of the city is without power for sixteen hours a day. There is supposed to be a schedule each week that will allow you to plan ahead, but the schedule changes daily, making it impossible to do the same things at the same time. Although Niti has a backup generator, it doesn't power the bedrooms. It's comical in a way; here we are in a gorgeous villa, and the power can cut out whenever and wherever.

Routine is a working bible for me, and snafus are a major issue. I resist change of any kind, not to mention being unable to adapt to new surroundings. Why would someone like me travel to a country so completely foreign in lifestyle and thinking? Well, wasn't that the plan? The one that teaches Ellie that yes, there is life—and often a happy one—beyond curled hair, makeup, fashion, real bathrooms, and little things like electricity? Which brings me to Big Red. Reflecting on landing in Bangkok without my twenty-two outfits, five pairs of shoes, 484 pills, and numerous bags of trail mix, I realize that I have worn less, eaten less, and taken but a handful of those essential vitamins. Electricity or not, the burning question remains: Did I really need to pack, drag, carry, lift, and lug so much stuff halfway around the world? The answer becomes more evident with each passing day.

CHAPTER TWENTY-FIVE

"She works hard for the money." ~ Donna Summer

May 14, Khokana and Bungamati, Kathmandu, Nepal

It's a clear, sunny day, and the temperature is rising when we head to Khokana, a Nepalese village of 5,000, just miles from the city. The countryside is tranquil against the curtain of the Himalayas, and I can see people tending their fields. We pass a sign for a Tibetan refugee camp. There are about 20,000 refugees throughout Nepal, and about 700 old men and women live in this camp. They were young when they left Tibet in the 1950s and early 1960s when their spiritual leader, the Dalai Lama, was forced into exile after a failed uprising against the Chinese. Keshar, my guide, explains that there are two religions in Nepal: Hinduism and Buddhism. The population numbers more than 26,000,000 from over one hundred ethnic groups, yet they coexist and often share the same temples and worship the same god albeit with different names. The religious tolerance and harmony in this country of millions is astounding. It should be a powerful example to the world. Each ethnic group, or caste, has its own distinct culture and traditions, making it a diverse melting pot that reminds me of New York City.

Keshar tells me about the village of Khokana, a Newari farming community so well-preserved that it's like traveling one hundred years back in time. The people live off the land, and many of their daily activities take place outside. Newari is spoken here.

Entering the village, which is little more than a main street with a couple of small side streets, feels like I'm in medieval times. Houses built in typical Newari style surround courtyards. Made of distinctive-looking mud bricks with straw or rice husks used as fillers, they are three stories tall, with sloped, tiled roofs. Wooden doors and windows are carved in a style rarely seen outside Nepal, and colorful garlands of red chilies hang between the villagers' laundry in the open air.

Passing the triple-tiered temple of Rudrayani, I notice several old men chitchatting away, with a couple of goats in the mix. In the courtyards we see women busy tending their children, goats, and sheep, preparing food, and filling buckets and cans with water from a tub or pipe sticking out of a building. I'm fascinated by the older women who use their hands and bare feet to spin yarn on wooden spinning wheels. There's rice in various stages of processing everywhere. When the rice in the paddies is ready, it is painstakingly cut with a sickle, an action that is repeated thousands of times. The bundles remain on the ground until they are brought back to the village.

The small, wiry women amaze me. Weighing less than a

hundred pounds soaking wet, they carry huge bundles of rice on their backs. They gather the shafts and beat them against the ground repeatedly for hours in the heat. Then the rice is left to dry on carpets in the sun for several days. The women stand on the carpets and do a twisting motion with their feet to remove the husks. The hulled rice is called *baji*, one of the most widely eaten foods in Nepal.

I sit on a step next to one woman and watch as she places the hulled rice in a large iron pan and stirs it over hot coals, careful not to burn it. No need for electricity here; a match is all that's required. She smiles and offers me a surprisingly tasty handful.

In the middle of the courtyard is a large well, several feet in diameter. Young children lean over the side and drop their buckets, fill them with water, then pull them back up. The women use the water to wash their clothing. The culture is so primitive that it is difficult to imagine being born into and living this lifestyle.

Khokana is well-known for its mustard seed oil, which is still made the traditional way. The men use heavy wooden beams to crush the seeds and extract the oil. The oil is used in cooking or for therapeutic massages. I'm struck by the disparity between our definition of prosperity and that of the Newari people. Who among us would be satisfied with fresh water, a bowl of baji, and a little mustard seed oil to soothe our weary bones?

We walk through old alleys and an archway flanked by two

large, stone lions to another tiny village, Bungamati. The homes are similar to the ones in Khokana. Corn and garlic hang from rafters, and there are blankets of grain and garlic drying in the sun. Women sit outside spinning, weaving, knitting, and going about their daily activities. An elder shows a young girl how to turn the grain, while other children sit among the mounds of hay and play on the temple steps among the worshippers.

Continuing on, we pass workshops, largely unchanged since the Middle Ages, where master wood-carvers and sculptors live and work. The men create items ranging from intricate moldings to extraordinary hand-carved masks. Watching these artisans craft each piece, I feel compelled to buy several gifts. Keshar makes sure that I barter to get the best price. Several times I make an offer, but the seller comes back with a no. When I walk away, as instructed by my guide, I hear the seller calling me back. If these sellers want to make a sale, they'll come after a potential buyer.

Food for thought: Everything I've bought so far has been handmade in Bhutan or Nepal. None of the labels say Made in

China except for my t-shirt and underwear purchases in Bangkok.

The Rato Machendranath Temple, built in 1857, sits in the center of the village square. Thought to be the birthplace of the god of rain and harvest who prevents drought during the rice season. His image is carved from a piece of red-painted wood with hand-drawn features and draped in flowers. It resides in this temple for six months of the year, then it's paraded around the city of Patan on a wheeled chariot. The icon is eventually brought back to Bungamati. Keshar says moving Rato Machendranath around is one of the most important festivals of the year.

Along the path are stones in the pavement decorated with paint that represent the footprints of Lakshmi, the goddess of wealth and prosperity. Making the most of a good opportunity, I stand on her footprints. It's a no-brainer compared to the worn footprints by Bhutan's squat holes.

Just as in Khokona, weaving between the villagers are dogs, goats, and ducks at every turn. They even prance or waddle in and out of the villagers' houses. The villagers keep track of their livestock by tying brightly colored ribbons to each, a sort of ID tag. Before we leave, I ask about the lack of tourists in these villages.

"Visitors are rare here," he replies. This surprises me because

the Newari people represent such an integral part of Nepal's cultural diversity.

Before we head back, we stop at a popular tourist area in Kathmandu called Thamel. The narrow alley-type streets are jam-packed with motorcycles, cars, and people. There are hotels and restaurants galore, along with yoga classes, pharmacies, and trekking shops for the thrill-seeking Everest climbers. On one street is a line of dental clinics. Outside one clinic I gawk at a twisted piece of wood with coins nailed to it—a toothache god, kissed by those coming and going.

Giggling quietly, I take in the unsightly teeth of the smiling locals and wonder who visits these clinics. There are vendors selling flutes, scarves, hippie pants, bangles, sari cloth, perfume, and beauty products—all in one of the poorest countries on Earth. Around every corner is a temple, shrine, or food market. Hardly a relaxing stroll surrounded by the hustle and constant beeping motorcycles. As we walk, Keshar tells me about Kathmandu's Freak Street—the famous street from the sixties and early seventies. Hippies from all over the world traveled to this street to purchase cannabis legally, and gain enlightenment. The allure ended when pot became illegal in the late seventies. Perhaps the Beatles were part of this landscape, and I'm reminded of Bhutan with its cannabis growing everywhere. Good thing it was an isolated country or it would have been a pot-smoking paradise.

The weathered, wrinkled faces of the hard-working Newari women are engraved in my mind. Day after day, under the heat of the sun, they carry those heavy bundles of rice and then twist the hulls off with their bare feet. And when the harvesting is done, they turn to scrubbing their clothes with a stone, in a bucket of water drawn from a deep well. Not a single woman is idle. It's clear that here a woman's work is truly never done. The men who do work seem to do a fair amount of nothing between tasks. Is there a gender gap when it comes to ease and relaxation as well?

I think about the conveniences that are supposed to make our lives stress-free: washers, dryers, dishwashers, refrigerators, freezers, cars, supermarkets, pharmacies, and shopping malls. How is it that stress is still so much a part of our daily lives?

In my room, I have some time before dinner to reorganize Big Red—again. Another flare of recognition—not one of these items will increase my life span or guarantee my happiness. While neatly folding my outfits, I'm unsure what it will take to change my behavior. I remove my unused Waterpik, suppressing a laugh. People here not only survive, but thrive in a civilization that has sustained itself with the barest necessities for thousands of years. And here I am, like some kind of spiritual-seeking imposter, with my massive suitcase filled to the brim with unnecessary stuff. Tonight as I climb into bed, I ponder the happiness factor. From what I've seen so far, I can only surmise that the gene exists here, at least in part. Perhaps it's because Nepal is a blend of so many indigenous ethnic groups. Laid-back, and seemingly content with what they have, the people's natural hospitality and strong sense of community offer a serene attitude that one does not find in the Western world. This is happiness in its most authentic form.

A quote from Espen Vidar says it best:

"Trying to find lasting happiness or contentment from better relationships, higher status, and more possessions was like drinking saltwater to quench your thirst."

Slowly, I begin to see that it can't be found in worldly trappings; happiness is an inside job.

In a half dream, I see myself at fourteen, working the tobacco fields as a summer job. I shudder to think of having to do that grueling work into old age. I would never survive, let alone have a smile on my face.

CHAPTER TWENTY-SIX

What's a little blood, sweat, and tears?

Ahh, manual labor, I am no stranger to it. I worked hard jobs, and always for the money.

At the age of ten, I had a large paper route, pedaling from one neighborhood to the next, six days a week, never missing a day no matter how bad the weather. Tips were like gold coins to me. At the end of each week I would spread out the pennies, nickels, and dimes on my bed and spend hours counting and recounting them. Every once in a while, a quarter or two would be hidden among the change, making me feel rich beyond measure. Each month I would carefully separate the coins, putting them into coin wrappers. I would run my fingers over the paper rolls with a tremendous sense of satisfaction. I would stash them away for safekeeping in one of my father's empty cigar boxes at the bottom of my dresser drawer until I had enough to buy something that I'd been yearning for.

After the newspaper route, I worked on a vegetable farm five miles from my house, walking both ways after school and in the early-morning hours on the weekends. Rain or shine, I toiled in those vegetable patches, weeding, watering, and eventually picking the crop. The pay wasn't much, and it was pretty dirty work, but it was enough to give me the incentive to keep working. As eighth grade came to a close, I heard about the tobacco farms where they paid more. It couldn't be any worse than the vegetable farm, I thought, so I signed up.

The first day just about did me in. Getting up at the crack of dawn, we rode a bus twenty-five miles across the state line into Connecticut. When we arrived, we were trained how to pick tobacco leaves. From then on it was eight hours working in the sweltering heat, crouched in an uncomfortable position to pick the lowest leaves. We would remove three from the plant on the right, then three from the one on the left. The leaves were made into bundles that were laid in the middle of the row. Later, a hauler would pick up the bundles and take them away. It was exhausting, back-breaking work, and the only means to prevent dehydration was by drinking salt water from the metal vats next to the outhouses.

The outhouse was my first experience in relieving myself in a despicable place. The thought of my rear end suspended over a noxious hole left me mortified. I had to prepare myself mentally before I entered. I'd take a deep breath and hold my hand over my mouth and nose. Forcing myself to look anywhere but down, I'd bend my knees and pray that time or something else would speed up. Who would have thought that this experience would follow me all the way to Asia so many years later?

The only shade was the cheesecloth netting over the tobacco plants. We sat and ate our lunch, unconcerned that the stains on our hands were caused by tar, the substance that prompted the warnings on today's cigarette packs. Getting back on the bus that first day, sweating like a pig, my clothes ruined by the sticky, brown tobacco stains, I had twenty-five miles to talk myself into never going back. That night, with the stink and sweat washed away in the shower, I could only think about that paycheck at the end of the week. I got up the next morning, and with the lunch my mother had packed, I stepped back on that bus.

Each day we would go from field to field picking leaves, returning to the same fields to pick the next layer. The cooler mornings weren't so taxing, but when noon arrived, the air under the nets was more than one hundred degrees on cloudless days. The endurance of the migrant tobacco pickers who worked the fields from sunrise to sundown amazed me.

When we were done with the field picking, the girls would head to the tobacco barns, where we stood at our benches, sewing the freshly picked leaves in pairs onto a string attached to a wooden rod. We did this until each rod was full, then placed it on the ground to be hung in rows between the rafters. We stood in one place and sewed for eight hours a day. Initially we suffered burns on our fingers from the string until we learned to wrap tape around our fingers and hands the way the experienced sewers did. I loved this part of the job, not only because I became a pretty skilled sewer, but because it was piecework. With each tobacco rod, I saw dollar bills flying into my pocket, money that would later be spent on the latest fad in clothing or makeup.

When the sewing was done, we had one more job to tackle. It involved going back into the heat of the fields to tie a cord around the big-leafed plants as they grew to the top of the netting. We would walk down the rows, gently twisting the cord around each plant. *Gently* was the operative word here, but by the end of the summer we were tired and dreaded the thought of looking at, never mind touching, one more tobacco leaf. So we made a pact that we would twist the cord on every other plant with just the right amount of tension to choke it. At $1.05 per hour, plus piecework, my salary was more than $40 a week. Not a bad take for eight weeks, so I continued to work the fields through blood, sweat, and tears for three more years.

After graduating from high school, with the tobacco fields permanently behind me, I chose to work on a sweat shop assembly line the year before I entered nursing school. This was another new experience for me. I sat for eight hours a day among hard-core factory workers, all women who had barely graduated from high school. We sat on cardboard boxes eating lunch with greasy hands and fingernails, watching the passing roach parade. Each evening when I clocked out, I had one word on my mind. *Quit.*

Various careers followed my twelve years as a pediatric nurse, from an adventure in sales to a roller-coaster ride up the corporate ladder. The years it took to earn the title of vice president replaced the blood and sweat with tremendous stress, but the tears remained. The fear of failure became a running theme in my life, but I worked through my fears and pushed onward. My experiences taught me not to be held hostage by fearful thinking and to face whatever task or situation I was presented with. As they say, I had it all, but as dramatic as the climb was, so was the fall.

I awoke one day with just one thought, to get out. Despite the monetary perks that allowed me to purchase whatever and whenever, and being held in high esteem in my field, it was crucial to my well-being to find a simpler way of life. I walked away from it all with no regrets and never looked back. On many fronts, the stage was being set for my *trip of a lifetime.*

I picture the men and women toiling day in and day out, and spot some similarities between us: jobs laborious in nature and the backbone to do what needs to be done. This is the only parallel to be drawn, for not only were my jobs temporary, each had one major purpose—to earn enough to acquire more stuff—while here the purpose is to eat a simple bowl of baji rice and end the day with a warm mustard oil massage.

Where will my peace, contentment, and happiness come from, and do I have the spiritual, and emotional, mettle to make the necessary changes?

CHAPTER TWENTY-SEVEN

Only one Jew?

May 15, Durbar Square, Patan, Nepal

Today we head to Patan—also known as Lalitpur—the oldest of the three royal cities in the valley. With a rich cultural history, it is home to 55 temples, and 136 monasteries. Situated in the center of the city is the famous Durbar Square. A former residence of Nepali royal families (*durbar* means palace), the complex is also the hub for Patan's religious and social life. The square—which dates to the twelfth century—is made up of three distinct temple courtyards and is a UNESCO World Heritage Site.

Words escape me as I admire the grand artistry of these ancient temples, although many of them include depictions of explicit erotic scenes and human sacrifices. Passing multicolor engravings on the walls and doors, I come face to face with one that sends a chill down my spine. In front of me is a large, red swastika.

Keshar notices my expression and to my relief tells me that it's a symbol of wealth and good fortune.

We stop to watch skilled artisans making and selling beaded jewelry, hand-carved masks, handmade paper, and painted greeting cards. We walk toward the Shiva-Parvati temple, where a group of children are playing badminton and Ping-Pong on a large stone slab with bricks in place of a net. Ingenious!

There are men dressed in robes in every color of the rainbow, their hair plaited in what looks like dreadlocks and sporting long beards. Their faces are painted in a variety of colorful patterns, each in a unique style. Keshar explains that they are Hindu holy men called *sadhus*. The sect to which they belong to is indicated by how they are adorned. Some wear only a loin cloth with a gold chain or bracelet; others wear nothing at all. Most sadhus are followers of the god Shiva. Homeless, they wander from place to place, living off the generosity of others. A sadhu sees me staring at him—fortunately he has clothes on—and asks if I want to take his picture. Keshar holds me back. "If you take his picture he will expect something in return." I decide to do it anyway and take a picture of this smiling Hindu holy man, and place three rupees in his outstretched hand, which is little more than a penny or two, if that. I'm embarrassed by the amount, but it was all the change I had. As we start to walk away, I hesitate and turn to look back. He is still standing there, watching me. He puts his hands together and bows his head in thanks, and I return the gesture. I wonder what a few pennies can buy. I think of all the times I have walked by a penny on the ground, too lazy to pick it up.

We stop for lunch at the Hotel Himalaya, overlooking one of the courtyards. I glance at the menu, but my stomach is doing flips. I ask Keshar what I should have. He chooses *dal*, a lentil soup served with a side of rice, a dish that's both delicious and safe. He orders *masu*, meat with curry spices with gravy and rice. He tells me Nepali people eat chicken, pork, and buffalo, but never beef because killing a cow in Nepal is prohibited.

Thrilled to discover that the restaurant has a bathroom, my excitement dissipates once I enter. It's the size of an airline restroom and has no toilet paper, and the smell is atrocious. I'm out of there in record time. This problem is following me around like a pesky fly.

After lunch, we stroll around, looking at the different temples, but one in particular stands out. Called the Golden Temple, it is a unique Buddhist monastery going back to the 1400s. Covered in copper-gilded siding, the large rectangular building is topped by three roofs. The main entrance, guarded by two golden lions, is always open as an invitation to all regardless of religion. A courtyard leads to the inner temple entrance, where we are greeted by two metal statues of elephants standing on tortoises. Between the elephants is an exquisitely carved doorway with Buddhas above it. After paying—this is the only temple we must pay to see—we remove our shoes and go inside, where we hear the harmonious chanting of the monks above us. Facing us are numerous gold and silver decorations, and a statue of a monkey with an almost-human gaze surrounded by gold prayer wheels. The focal point of the main shrine is a golden Buddha. Two bells hang from the ceiling in front of him. As we leave, we pass more golden doors, windows, and gates. Sadly, I discover that most of the temple is polished brass, not gold.

Although we have done a lot of walking, I try to resist feeling tired. Our final stop is the Patan Museum, the major attraction in Durbar Square. The museum doors—guarded by two stone lions—are embellished with gilt copper and inscriptions dating back to 1854. One of the finest museums in South Asia, it has more than 900 exhibits, and is home to many sacred art objects including some rare ones. Most the exhibits are sculptures of Hindu and Buddhist deities created in the Kathmandu Valley, many in the nearby workshops of Patan. Others come from India, Tibet, and the western Himalayas. The exhibits are designed to help viewers understand the living culture outside the museum's walls.

In the first gallery there are images of deities who can be identified by the way they sit or stand or by their clothing, whether they have multiple heads and limbs, how their hands are positioned, and what they are holding. My head is spinning. I can't even begin to keep up with Keshar's explanations about who's who or what's what. His English is a challenge for me to follow, plus my brain is fried from trying to process so much information. As we walk from gallery to gallery, I begin to tune him out and find myself wondering about his life here and his job as a guide. I think about how many tourists like myself, with and without all the baggage, he must escort through his country, being patient and always courteous. I stay at his side through several galleries as he tries to educate me. We stop on the second floor in front of some deep bay windows with cushioned seats. Sitting, we look out at the incredible views of the square below. Outside, crowds of tourists meander through the tranquil courtyards or visit the different temples and stupas while the locals go about their daily routines. It truly is a living museum.

This was worth the visit, but I look forward to just hanging out in Niti's fragrant garden, enjoying the peace and quiet.

On the car ride back, Keshar announces that there is one Jew in the area. I think, *Is this really possible, just one Jew?* Feeling lonesome at this stage of the trip, I want to blurt out, *Take me to him; he is one of my people.* You see, my father was Jewish. Now you can understand my gut reaction to that swastika. Finally, I ask, "One Jew, Keshar? Only one?"

He replies, "Oh yes, just one Jew."

I sit back and ponder this for a few moments and think, *How can there be only one Jew in a population of almost a million people?* It makes no sense. Leaning forward, careful not to seem impolite, I ask, "Why is there only a single Jew in all of Kathmandu? There has to be more than one."

Keshar confirms, "Yes, only one, the Patan Jew."

That's when the lightbulb comes on. "Oh, *zoo*," I say, sitting back, trying hard not to burst out laughing. "Now *that* makes perfect sense."

CHAPTER TWENTY-EIGHT

Anointed with a bindi and a flower

May, 16, Bhaktapur, Nepal

Today we will visit the artisan town of Bhaktapur, known as the city of devotees. A little trivia: the movie *Little Buddha* was filmed here. A typical Newari village, it is shaped like a conch shell. The major attractions are the ancient Hindu temples, palaces, stone statues, and Buddhist monuments. You encounter images of various deities at every turn. The royal palace here has a beautifully carved golden gate made of brass and embellished with monsters and mythical creatures.

In front of the gate is a statue of the ancient king Bhupatin-dra Malla mounted on a stone pillar. His arms are folded as if he is admiring the entrance to his palace. A large bell that hangs over the king's head is rung twice a day in honor of a goddess. Next to it is the Barking Bell—when it rings all the dogs start whining and barking. What else will follow me from Bhutan?

Inside the gate, I crane my neck skyward, taking in the five-story, pagoda-style, Nyatapola Temple, which at a height of ninety feet is the tallest temple in Nepal. Called the window palace, it has fifty-five ornate, hand-carved teak windows, including the famous peacock window, aka the Mona Lisa of Nepal.

Next, we come to the famous Lion Gate. Inside is a school, and it's thought that the lions keep students from skipping school. If only that were all we needed to keep students from being truant back home.

Walking the perimeter of the square, you get a close-up view of artisans producing a variety of handcrafts. I watch them working on their *thangka*, or scroll paintings. Tibetan in origin, they depict everything from Buddhist gods to famous scenes from the life of Buddha. One of the more popular subjects is the Wheel of Life, which portrays the teachings of enlightenment. It takes almost six years to learn the many painting techniques while studying the religious texts on which the motifs are based. That is followed by five to ten years to become an expert in this art form. In addition to being used for teaching purposes, the thangkas are hung to overcome sickness and hardships, and to bring protection and blessings into peoples' homes. Definitely an alternative to the Divine Mad Monk's thunderbolt.

There's a wide range of prices, and the ones with real gold detail are priced beyond my comfort zone. After bartering for a while, I purchase a handsome piece with a touch of gold that depicts the life of Buddha.

Moving on, we come to a stall where big slabs of raw meat—surrounded by flies—are being carved into pieces. There's a large glass half filled with the blood they have drained from the flesh and a pile of bones to the side. I watch as they wrap the raw meat in paper, capturing a few lucky flies inside each package. I try to forget the extra fly topping before my appetite disappears for good. I have continued to lose weight, which means Big Red gets harder to budge with each passing day. I need to marshal my strength or get serious about lightening her load, and soon.

The smell of clay baking in the sun wafts through the air as we approach Pottery Square. Rows of small gray and reddish-brown pots seem to go on forever. Made from different kinds of earthenware, they are laid outside to dry. Each potter has his or her own job; some shape the clay on traditional wooden wheels, while others pound the bottoms to make them smooth and flat. Every task is performed with a certain rhythm and sound. Together they create an orchestral background for the chanting of the potters. Each one is examined by weather-beaten hands before being turned to face into the sun. The process runs like a finely tuned assembly line.

Heading back, we spot a queue of locals waiting to be blessed by a holy man tucked inside a temple doorway. Handing me some rupees, Keshar encourages me to join the line. Walking up the steps, I timidly approach the holy man holding out my offering. Speaking in a language I don't understand, he places a tiny flower behind my ear, dips his thumb in some red powder, then dabs it in the center of my forehead, offering me a toothless smile. The red powder, or *bindi*, on my forehead is both a blessing and protection. I try to preserve it while carefully wiping the sweat from my face, but my bindi soon looks more like war paint.

On our return drive, I look over the notes I've taken since arriving in Kathmandu. Together with my Bhutan adventures, they are mind-blowing. I need to capture some of the highlights on my blog, where my following has grown since I left the US. Not only am I hearing from family and friends, but also from followers in the US, Europe, and Japan.

Back in my room, I prepare Red for our escape to the jungle—a welcome change from the procession of temples that I've visited. I relax in the little chair by my bed, trying to wind down. I find myself making a comparison between bindis and the ashes on the first day of Lent. The ashes are a sign of mourning and repentance, while the bindi signifies a blessing and protection. There is no question which I prefer. To be protected and blessed is a heavenly combination.

Smiling, I slip off my shoes. So far, I have been blessed by a bow and arrow, a wooden replica of the Divine Mad Monk's penis, and a bindi. I should fear nothing for the rest of my journey. We shall see.

CHAPTER TWENTY-NINE

Finally, a successful squat!

May 17, Kathmandu, Nepal

Asian Pacific Adventures arranged for a side trip to the Royal Chitwan National Park, located in the forests and grasslands in the foothills of the Himalayas. Going on a safari fulfills another dream of mine and is a perfect complement to my Asian journey. My travel agent mentioned that Hollywood stars, VIPs, and dignitaries have visited here. Richard Gere's name came up, so how can I resist? Sign me up!

I will soon eat those words.

Today I leave Kathmandu and fly to the jungle, where I will go on a safari, take nature walks and drive through the jungle, and bird-watch, all accompanied by experienced naturalists. I am ready for another grand adventure; my excitement is palpable.

The travel agency prepared me well for my jungle stay. I carefully packed SPF 50 sunscreen, lip balm, long-sleeve shirts, jeans, hats, insect repellent, and that half-gallon jug of Permethrin spray to protect me from dengue fever. The latter, along with everything else, has been carted all the way from home and helped tip the scales, costing me a hundred dollars in excess baggage fees. Although I've been vaccinated for any possible diseases, there is no vaccine for dengue fever, an acute febrile disease transmitted by mosquitoes, but contracting this disease is merely a passing concern. After all, I have my Permethrin to protect me. Unsure of what clothing I should take, I opted to pack extra; after all, who knows what one will need in a jungle? Check in with me later.

May 17, Kathmandu airport/ Nepali jungle

Par for the course, this trip continues to test my strength, resolve, and fortitude. Dropped off at the Kathmandu airport, I must navigate my way alone. By now I fear stepping into an airport. I'm apprehensive about getting lost, not finding the right gate, or repeating my German airport debacle. I'm certainly not looking forward to another scene with this ridiculously over-packed suitcase. Passing through the twelfth airport, the lighten-the-load mantra has taken up permanent residence in my head. Finding my gate—not hard since there are only two—I plunk down on a chair in the front and decide not to budge until departure unless I absolutely *must* use the restroom.

The word *restroom* is an oxymoron. I find no rest in any kind of bathroom, especially the Far East version of squat and drop. Unfortunately, I have to go. Dragging Big Red, I know full well she'll never fit through the door, so I leave her outside—no one would try to steal her; one tug and they'd stop dead. I could check her at my departure gate, but I want to get this over with quickly. Resolute, my roll of 3-ply in hand, I take a deep breath, enter, and face the notorious hole surrounded by cement. Cringing, just the sight of it makes my stomach churn. Will I finally accept my fate and squat over the hole? I've held out for fourteen days at this point; what's one more day? But this time I have no choice. Holding the door shut eliminates my fear of being seen as a novice squatter. Pulling down my cream-colored capris—not the smartest choice of clothing for this activity—I gingerly straddle the hole. Placing my feet carefully, I try not to squat too far forward to prevent any splash back. Clinging for dear life onto the door, my squat results in a perfect bull's-eye. Not bad for a newbie. Clearly, all facets of life hang in *the balance*. Just as Eastern philosophy proclaims, a sense of balance is essential for ease and contentment; so too with a successful squat. Maybe not the best analogy, but isn't it interesting how one can find pearls of wisdom in the strangest places?

Heading back to the departure gate, I see the tiny prop plane that will take me to Bharatpur. Hauling Big Red behind me, I begin to fret that I'll have to unload some of my stuff before I check her at the gate. Luckily, Big Red is accepted as is, but not without some curious stares. Everyone else has a backpack or small carry-on. It's increasingly evident that I must do more than *consider* lightening Red's load. With many more miles to cover and places to see, I need to decide what can be jettisoned and be done with it.

Excited about my jungle adventure, I deplane, collect Big Red, and pull/roll/drag her into the terminal to find my driver, a man with a broad smile and my name on a sign. His initial eagerness to take Red off my hands turns that big smile upside down as he discovers her weight. I expect I will see a picture of Red on a poster soon with the headline: Warning! Approach at your own risk!

I follow him to the Jeep that will take me to the Paradise Resort. I gape at what is supposed to be my transportation. My shocked expression has to be right up there with my first encounter with a toilet pit. At first glance, the outside of the vehicle isn't so bad, but the inside looks as if it had been torched. There is no dash-board, just a bunch of exposed wires trailing from the driver's side to the passenger side. The word *filthy* cannot begin to describe its condition. Once again my white blouse and cream-colored capris are not appropriate apparel. I'm getting more enlightened at every turn. Getting in, I don't know where to sit or what to lean up against; all options are equally bad.

As we bump along in the intense heat—air-conditioning is

a moot point since there are no windows—I keep my arms and legs glued to my torso to avoid touching any part of the vehicle. Feeling a little crabby, I should never have asked how long our ride will take. How did this wind up as part of my trip package?

Jouncing along, we pass women walking barefoot in the heat, carrying babies in the front and huge sacks on their backs. Sweaty and a little less pristine, I decide to go with the flow. By the time we arrive, my demeanor has softened. Ahh, Buddhism at its best.

CHAPTER THIRTY

Welcome to paradise?

I did a lot of research in preparation for this trip, not only about the Three Kingdoms, but also about the hotel accommodations. I'm a fanatic about making sure my room is spacious and has all the amenities, including room service, movies on demand, etc. After all, your hotel is your home away from home. On this trip, I was told not to expect five-star accommodations. I read on the resort's website that it had just undergone extensive renovations and was designed with all the modern amenities and services. "Close to two decades of experience has taught us what is important to our guests—everything! We intend to make your stay a paradise. We provide all the creature comforts and services of the modern world. The Paradise Resort is arguably one of the best destinations for those seeking an enthralling jungle experience." Their words came back to taunt me.

May 17, Paradise Resort, Chitwan National Park, Nepal

Greeted by a resort employee who offers me a much-needed wet towel and a cold drink on arrival, I take in my surroundings, acutely aware of how quiet it is. I assume the other guests must be out taking part in one of the many jungle activities. Sipping my drink in the sweltering heat, I glance at a huge blackboard that lists the activities for the day. Underneath each activity is a space to list the guests who will be participating. The elephant safari ride, scheduled for 4:30 P.M., has one name written under it, mine. Puzzled, I ask the gentleman behind the bar, "Will anyone be joining me?"

"No," he answers with a smile.

I ask warily, "Am I the only one here?"

"Yes," he responds.

"Just for today?" I ask.

"No," he says.

"You mean for my entire stay? I'm the only guest here?"

"Yes" is the response.

I sit back on the bench, slightly alarmed. This doesn't make sense.

"Why?" I ask in disbelief.

Response: "This is not the tourist season. It gets so hot here and there are lots of mosquitoes at this time of year."

I walk away shaking my head.

So, it will be just me, the lone potential victim for millions of blood-sucking mosquitoes. One consolation is that I am armed with that 30 percent Deet mosquito spray, along with my jug of Permethrin. I wanted to make this trip alone; apparently the universe is granting my wish.

I check into my room—more about that later—and change for my elephant ride. I undress and carefully spray the mosquito repellent over every square inch of my body, almost asphyxiating myself, a reminder that *less is more* and *common sense* have never been my strong points. I put on my long-sleeve shirt and carefully tuck the hem of my jeans securely inside my socks—my one-and-only jungle-appropriate outfit. Reaching for the Permethrin spray that will protect me from those dreaded dengue fever mosquitoes, something tells me to read the label first.

CAUTION! Harmful if swallowed, inhaled or absorbed through the skin. Do not get in the eyes or on the skin. Avoid breathing in vapors or spray mist. Exposure may induce adverse effects on the nervous system. Ingestion may result in vomiting.

The list goes on to include a warning that this toxic stuff is also highly flammable. I read on.

Repellent should be applied outdoors before clothing is worn; hang out clothing, spray and let dry for several hours.

Sitting on the bed, I mull over my dilemma. I had gone to a lot of trouble and expense to purchase this jug of Permethrin and traveled more than 7,500 miles with this *must have* stuffed inside Big Red, and it never once crossed my mind to read the damned directions. What a waste. With a disgusted grunt I put the useless jug on the dresser and opt to take my chances and go without. My elephant awaits. Walking down the path, I mutter to myself, "Dengue fever or convulsions, dengue fever or convulsions. I'll take my changes with the fever."

CHAPTER THIRTY-ONE

"In the jungle, the mighty jungle, the lion sleeps tonight"
~ "The Lion Sleeps Tonight" by Linda Solomon

At last, the long-awaited Elephant Safari Ride, where I will see lions, and tigers, and what, oh my! I have a dramatic vision of the elephant scooping me up with its trunk and deftly placing me on its back, just like in the circus. I'm somewhat disappointed to see a large platform atop a tall scaffolding. The elephant calls to me as it awaits my arrival. Climbing up the scaffolding, I step onto the platform with the help of my *mahout*,

or elephant driver. He tells me her name is Mumbai as I cautiously step into the basket secured to her back. He situates me close to the elephant's head, straddling her with my legs, which are hanging out the sides of the basket. It almost seems as if he is trying to ensure that all 100 pounds of me can keep the entire basket balanced atop this lightweight of 12,000 pounds. *Not possible*, I think with amusement and doubt, but he is so intent on making sure I am secure and safe that I don't worry.

All settled in—the mahout straddling Mumbai's neck, his feet secure in rope stirrups, and I pretty much balanced in the basket—we lurch our way into the jungle. I have an adrenaline rush and want to pinch myself. I'm riding a real elephant into a real jungle. But the sensation disappears rather quickly as I try to balance myself, prepare to be camera-video-ready, and swat away swarming mosquitoes all at the same time. Adjusting my cameras, I fear—despite my backup batteries—that I won't have enough power to capture everything. To have my equipment quit in an exotic jungle with 43 species of mammals, 450 species of birds, and 45 species of amphibians—many endangered— would kill me. In retrospect, I needn't have worried. Equipment failure will prove to be the least of my concerns over the course of our four-hour trek. My biggest issue: keeping the mosquitoes from eating me alive.

Thirty minutes into our slow, lumbering ride I see what looks like a monarch butterfly. I don't reach for the camera or binoculars by my side. No need to disrupt the weight balance for that. After all, there is so much more to capture on video. Meanwhile, my mahout is constantly on the lookout, standing upright in the stirrups, one hand over his eyes, searching far into the distance. As time ticks by, we proceed at an elephant's pace. Hanging on to the basket with one hand and swatting mosquitoes with the other, I begin to think we're only going to see jungle, jungle, and more jungle.

Suddenly, he makes Mumbai stop, saying excitedly, "Look, look!"

Leaning forward with anticipation and fumbling for my

camera, I strain to see what he is pointing at. In the distance along the banks of the river, I make out something that looks like a rock. Can't be that. "Where, where?" I ask. He repeats, "Look, look!" As the river water ripples, the shape seems to move; lo and behold, what appears is the snout of a crocodile. Since he is getting so excited I squeal in delight but decline to snap a picture.

It takes another hour before he gets all fired up again and proceeds to yell, "Look, look!"

Grabbing my cameras, I strain to see what he's pointing at this time. There it is, a spotted deer. A beautiful spotted deer, but a deer nonetheless. Again I don't want to hurt his feelings, so I cry out "Amazing," hoping I sound believable. He turns, looks at me, and commands, "Take a picture." I snap a few photos to humor him. In his now-standing position, hand over his eyes, he continues searching, searching, searching. He suddenly shouts, "Look, look, three, three!"

"Oh my God, three what?" I ask. I try to hoist myself up, not easy after sitting immobile, straddling an enormous elephant for almost two hours. Sure enough, there are three: three more spotted deer. I guess correctly that he will not move that elephant until I take another picture.

Over the next hour we see at least thirty more spotted deer. How do I know how many? My mahout counts each one, and I must take a picture of them. By the fifteenth deer I pretend to snap pictures. I certainly don't want to offend my guide, but I won't run down my batteries taking picture of an animal that is neither near extinction nor unusual. Besides, my body can no longer take the twisting and stretching as I try to see around Mumbai's huge head. Past fifteen I stop acting excited and simply respond, "Yeah, wow, yeah." Come to find out, these spotted deer are often seen in herds of thirty to fifty and sometimes number up to one hundred. I will be forever grateful we encountered smaller numbers.

I start to get so bored that I begin taking selfies while my mahout performs his standard hand-to-forehead search. With my eyes closed, I have an *aha* moment. I can use the picture I just took of my face and put it on t-shirts and coffee mugs—the ideas are endless. I might make a few bucks selling these by claiming this is an original photograph of the strangest and perhaps rarest never-to-be-seen-again animal in the Nepali jungle. T-shirts, mugs, anyone?

I am startled out of my entrepreneurial reverie when my guide screams, "Look, look." I follow his pointed finger down to a huge pile of shit. But this isn't just any old pile of shit. Apparently this dump was left by an exotic one-horned rhino. I gotta tell you, after monarch butterflies, too many deer, and a croc's nose, I am ecstatic. This could be my only proof that I was really in the jungle, and I want to capture this important scene for posterity. Unfortunately, to my guide, this is just a pile of crap and not picture worthy, so he keeps Mumbai moving. I try to take the picture by turning around, but it's impossible to keep your balance on a moving elephant. Clearly, we are not on the same wavelength when it comes to what's important to capture on film. One man's treasure is another man's shit or something like that.

Disappointed, I face forward as he leads our elephant down to the banks of the Rapti River. I must mention here that my mahout doesn't seem to be the greatest elephant driver, because he can't keep this big lug of a beast on one path. Of course, staying on a path is not a problem for elephants. No path, no problem, they just create one, no matter how dense the vegetation is. Indeed, staying on the path does not appear to trouble my guide either. Seated on the elephant's neck, he is in a better position to avoid the brush and branches we encounter. He has a long steel goad in his hands that he uses to push aside anything blocking our way. Most of the time, he leaves it to Mumbai to uproot it. Going down unbeaten paths is becoming an issue, because my legs are getting banged and battered. But what the hell are a few bruises, torn jeans, and the possibility of my femurs being dislocated? After all, I'm on a jungle safari halfway around the world, and so far I have seen a butterfly, a croc's nose, thirty deer, and a pile of rhino flop.

At one point, we interrupt the *adventure* to stop near an opening in the jungle that dips down to the river's bank. Paying no attention to me, my mahout slides off the elephant and runs out onto a narrow tree floating in the river. I'm left atop Mumbai, swatting away squadrons of mosquitoes. If anything, that heavy-duty spray I used seems to be attracting more than repelling. Struck by another *aha* moment, I begin to contemplate beekeepers apparel. Not a single part of your body would be exposed to the elements, and those bee veils would look quite fetching with one of my wide-brim hats. After twenty minutes, my mahout scoops something out of the water and runs back holding an exquisite bright-pink lotus flower. Thinking it's for me, I anticipate taking it in my hands. It's been said that a lotus flower's beauty rising from the muddy water suggests our own spiritual potential and that no matter how long we have lived in the muck, our innate beauty is always present within us. Regrettably this gift of nature isn't intended for me. I guess the generosities of Buddha do not apply in the jungle.

In slow motion, we approach the steep slope down to the Rapti because Mumbai is thirsty. Going down steep embankments is a breeze for an elephant, but imagine what it's like being on top of one. The basket tilts at such an angle that I feel as if I'm about to be shot out of a cannon. Sticky with sweat and mosquito spray, I wish that I could cool myself off. Mumbai steps into the river and keeps right on going, I'm about to learn that elephants take their time drinking. Since she is in no hurry, I just sit high up on her back in this wide river and close my eyes, relishing this peaceful moment. It doesn't last. Mumbai suddenly lifts her trunk and drenches me with the spray of all sprays. She repeats this several times. I got my wish.

I got cooled off, and so did my perfectly styled hair.

As we head back to the resort, I'm a little disappointed that we haven't seen any lions or tigers, or anything else of much interest. Unexpectedly, my guide brings Mumbai to a halt, turns to me, and whispers, "Look to your right." I am awestruck. There it is, up close and personal: an elusive, one-horned rhino surrounded

by some rhesus monkeys. The rhino is huge, brownish gray, with thick skin folds that give it an armor-plated appearance. It looks like a tank with short, skinny legs. I take my picture, a perfect way to end the day.

But it's not over yet. My guide asks if I want to ride Mumbai back to home base. I assume he means for me sit behind him on the elephant's neck. Although this isn't on my bucket list of things to do before I die, being in the moment, I respond with a yes.

I don't have a chance to rethink my answer because he has already slid off the elephant and is telling me to sit on Mumbai's neck. I clumsily duck and crawl between the bars of the basket and get myself astride her neck. I try to gain some support by putting my feet in the rope stirrups, but my legs are too short.

That's when I realize my guide is making no attempt to rejoin me. I assume he's going to use a rope to lead Mumbai back. No. He hands me the elephant goad he used. Unnerved, I have no idea how to direct an elephant, with or without an elephant goad. This was definitely not listed in my travel itinerary under must-do. Clinging to Mumbai's neck, I lean down to hand the guide my camera so he can take my picture. This must be captured for the record books. How impressed will the folks back home be?

The picture taken, I wait for him to lead the way. Instead he jogs a few feet ahead, snaps one more picture, then takes off running, *with* my camera. *Are you kidding me?* What kind of

guide abandons a tourist in the middle of a jungle, let alone one sitting atop a 12,000-pound elephant? How the hell am I supposed to find my way out? Fear washes over me. I blow out a series of short breaths. My mind is busy cataloging the possible dangers. What if the elephant gets spooked by one of those as yet unseen Bengal tigers or a sloth bear or a jackal? What if I fall off and get trampled? Surely the guy is coming back?

After a while, my so-called guide still nowhere to be seen, I realize I am alone. Totally alone. On top of a huge beast. In the middle of nowhere. Feel free to laugh if you want. Petrified and fuming, I have no option other than to cling to the elephant's neck and try to find our way back. As we move forward, I pray that Mumbai has the way committed to memory. Elephants never forget, right? I dearly hope that this one doesn't.

Something tells me sitting upright and maintaining balance is key. Instead I'm half on, half off her neck, grasping her long strands of hair as we go down a steep hill. Holding on with a life-or-death grip, my legs flailing against her sides, I pray Mumbai won't lose her footing. Ever so slowly, we make our way out of the jungle. I can't say unharmed though; my shoulder is screaming.

As we approach the elephant's home base, I gain a bit of confidence until an image of an overstuffed Big Red flashes before my eyes. How am I going to continue lifting, lugging, and dragging her until my *trip of a lifetime* comes to an end? I no longer need Ron's "way to heavy" flitting through my brain. My arm, with a potential torn rotator cuff, is all the reminder I need. It's time to start unloading. At last I know what I can part with. But first things first.

Seeing the guide standing on the scaffolding waiting for us, I wonder if his desertion was a preplanned part of the adventure for the benefit of naive visitors to brag about back home? Mumbai gracefully backs into the scaffolding. Swinging my spent legs over her neck, I drop to the scaffolding and make my way down the ladder. I think for a moment about questioning the mind-set of my guide, but since I've survived, I chalk it up to a true *once* in lifetime experience. I retrieve my cameras and start back to my room when I hear a loud, gushing sound. I turn to see Mumbai, in the true spirit of graciousness, has waited until I am far enough away before she lets it rip. Elephants don't have to worry about where *they* will relieve themselves.

CHAPTER THIRTY-TWO

Paradise Lost

May 18, Paradise Resort, Chitwan National Park, Nepal

Before I tell you about my final day in the jungle, I want to share with you how things operate here in Paradise—the resort—and my room with no TV and no phone. So much for the modern amenities touted in the resort literature.

Next to the door in my room is a huge sign. It covers several things but focuses on one main topic: fire. It lists everything you need to do in case of a fire, such as let your neighbors know, and do not go back for any belongings. I thought the emphasis on fire odd, but not as vexing as being told the electricity will be turned off at 11 P.M. No lights, no air, no nothing. Sleeping should be just great at ninety-five degrees, plus humidity. I guess electricity is not considered a modern convenience here in Paradise.

I did remember to bring my loofa and my pineapple-coconut bath gel, essential must-haves for the jungle; but a flashlight—why would I bring one of those?

As soon as I was informed of the electricity situation, I asked for a flashlight so I could find my way to the bathroom in the dark. Response: "No flashlights, madam, only candles." Obviously this is why the fire warning is highlighted on the posted list of instructions.

I think most people can attest that it's not uncommon to become disoriented trying to locate the bathroom or anything else in a strange room in the middle of the night. Even though the bathroom is just a few feet from the bed, I want to be prepared. So the first night, while we still had electricity, I did several dry runs with a lit candle, going back and forth. I put one of the candles and the matches on the bedside table. With my eyes closed to simulate darkness, I fumbled around for the matches. Eyes still closed, I unsuccessfully tried to light the match several times. I was beginning to get skittish. It was nearing the magic hour of eleven when the electricity would be cut. I lay in bed, trying to relax and take my mind off the family of geckos scattered on the walls, ceiling, and floor, along with the insects patrolling the perimeter of the room. Earlier I had the pleasure of watching them have a field day in the shower and sink. I looked over at the huge jug of Permethrin on a shelf not far from the bed, and it gave me pause. Did I really want to risk getting up in the dark, attempt to reach for a candle, and fumble to light it in a room with a half-gallon jug of highly flammable stuff just a few feet away? I don't think so.

To make certain I would sleep through the night and not have to use the bathroom, I opened my bottle of Ambien and took twice the normal dose. I turned off the lights, and as I drifted off to sleep, I had one last thought. Far better to become addicted to sleeping pills than to die in a fire.

I should mention here that I loathe insects of any kind. Before I got into bed that first night, I had one more act to perform: attempting to stomp out as many insects as I could see. The geckos were a different matter. I did the only thing possible. Despite sweating like a pig, I wound my entire body within the sheets, giving myself just enough space to breathe, grateful that the extra dose of Ambien would put me in a coma in case one of them slithered into my cocoon. The letting-go test has reached its apex.

At 5 A.M., there was a knock on my door—my wake-up call. Today is another safari day, this time in a nice, comfortable Jeep.

Keeping to my word to lighten the load, I gather my stock-
pile of candies, trail mix, cookies, and crackers before I go
to the dining hall. Common sense should tell me that these
items probably weigh a pound total if that. But hey, it's a start.
Goodies in hand, off I go.

You know the old saying: I hate to eat alone. The true impact
comes across when you're eating in a room that will hold one
hundred, and ninety-nine are missing. This is how I have every
meal in Paradise. The good thing about being the only one is,
no one stares at you or feels sorry for you. The heat is already
rising, and the servers are kind enough to put a tall, upright fan
in front of me. Since I'm the only guest at the resort, air-conditioning is not an option. Welcome to Paradise!

By six o'clock, my guide/driver and I are walking over to the
Jeep. To my dismay, it is the same filthy one I rode here in,
only this time I get to sit in the back. Riding through the hot,
humid jungle, the nonstop bouncing torments my body. By
the end, my sides, arms, and hands are sore from trying to keep
myself from falling out. On a positive note, my ass is still numb
from yesterday's elephant ride. Yay!

Do we see lions, tigers, or bears? Nope. Not a one. Not even a
white-spotted deer, butterfly, croc snout, or one-horned rhino.
I tell the guide several times to turn around and go back, but
he only knows one direction—forward. It obviously doesn't
matter that I've reached the end of my rope; we keep going.
Slowly, I start to dispose of my goodies. I see this as being beneficial on two fronts. One: Big Red has shed one whole pound.
Two: Maybe, just maybe, my path of M&Ms, trail mix, and
crackers will entice something to come out of hiding.

Two hours into this jungle trek and I've seen nothing except a
group of soldiers patrolling for rhino poachers. From what my
guide tells me, every rhino organ carries some impressive value.
The horn is ground up and fetches from $10,000 to $60,000.
Believed to be an aphrodisiac, it's also used to treat fevers and

convulsions. Rhino dung is used as a laxative, and the urine is supposed to cure tuberculosis and asthma. The blood is said to cure menstrual problems. Everything is sold on the black market. My guide starts to tell me how the poachers dig big holes for the rhinos to fall into. I ask him to stop right there.

After three hours of nonadventure, my tired, aching body is jounced back to base camp. I will leave after lunch for a two-hour nature walk, *if* I can walk. This will give me another perspective of the jungle. Maybe now I will have my great wildlife experience. I had been told that the short grass makes February through May the best season to see the animals. I was also told that the key to enjoying the game park is patience. Well, I've been more than patient since I got here. This is it, folks. My last opportunity to see lions and tigers and whatever else might jump out at me. Seems like I might have to invent some stories to tell back home. I wonder if my expectations are being dashed as part of a big and not-so-amusing lesson the Universe is constantly trying to teach me: let it go, Ellie.

CHAPTER THIRTY-THREE

Trekking in the deep, dark, scary jungle

May 18, Paradise Resort, Chitwan National Park, Nepal

In preparation for our hike, the guide informs me the trails are not marked, and the wildlife can be dangerous. At this point, I want to yell, "Who cares about danger, just let me see something, anything wild!" About ten minutes into the walk, the guide turns and says we need to be quiet so we won't frighten the animals. I fight the urge to make a sarcastic crack like "What animals?" but force myself to remember the whole notion of respecting others. That's when his cell phone goes off. A cell phone in the jungle? Something is not right here.

Chitwan is known as a paradise for bird-watchers, and my guide attempts to point out quite a few exotic birds; but I can never see what he's pointing at. I keep asking, "Where, where?" This trek is beginning to have a familiar ring to it.

As we move farther into the jungle, I spot something I think must be exotic. I take my guide's cue and begin to point and exclaim, "Over there, over there!" Straining to see what I'm pointing at, he comes back with "Where, where?" He finally follows my finger and informs me that it is the rear end of a chicken with its head in the ground. A chicken's ass on my exotic jungle trek? No pictures, please!

Walking along a well-worn path, my guide points out some interesting plants. One, called a touch-me-not, folds its leaves in as soon as you touch it, then, after a few seconds, unfolds them again. There is also a plant called stinging nettles. The guide points to one growing on the side of the narrow path. As I bend down to get a closer look, he warns me not to touch it. They have stinging hairs like little hypodermic needles. If you brush against one, it releases an acid onto your skin that causes swelling and a painful burning and itching sensation. He tells me that despite their fearsome reputation, the nettle has many uses. Apparently when cooked it tastes like spinach, and get this: you can wash your hair in a nettle-based shampoo to get rid of dandruff. You can drink it as tea or, better yet, make nettle beer or wine. Get drunk enough and who cares about a little burning, swelling, or itching.

It turns out these two unusual plants are not so unusual. They can be found in abundance back home in the States—but by now I'm grasping at straws trying to find something out of the ordinary!

At this point this three-hour jungle adventure has been nothing to brag about. All I can say for certain is what an Asian chicken's ass looks likes when it's pointing toward the sky. Nary a lion or tiger the entire time. Mosquitos though numbered in the millions. Sigh.

We stroll along the outskirts of the jungle to a village where the Tharu tribe lives. Made up of about 28,000 people, some say they are descendants of Buddha. They have lived here for hundreds of years and call themselves the people of the forest. Working as farmers and peddlers, they live hand to mouth in huts built of mud and grass, with thatched roofs and no windows. They have large, open front porches where most of their daily activities take place. To keep the huts cool in the summer, they put animal dung in the building mix. Not so fascinating or interesting is the fact that wherever I walk I not only see plenty of dung, I step in plenty as well. I know one pair of sandals I will be leaving behind with no regrets!

The Tharu women have great respect for guests and are quite hospitable. I am invited to enter one of their small houses: honestly a midget would feel tall in there. Stooping over, I feel as if I'm walking into a dark cave. Mud walls partition the one big room. The kitchen is no more than five feet wide, with a deep hole in the middle for indoor cooking. I notice a lightbulb dangling from a wire, but it's not on. The Tharus are famous for their clean houses. Even though the floors are made from mud and their goats, chickens, and an occasional cow meander in and out, the house is immaculate, with no sign of animal droppings. Exiting, I notice one of the women cooking rice over an open fire. Standing close beside her is a little girl holding up what looks to be a dead animal. I am graciously offered a taste of the rice, but I decline, unsure of what else might have gone into the bowl. The village and its inhabitants are the most fascinating part of the entire trek.

Heading back, we meet up with a herd of bleating goats that follow us. Scampering all around us is one little, white goat attempting to keep up. I delight in this simple encounter. In the vast fields in the distance are villagers in wooden carts pulled by oxen. I remember reading that oxen represent the powerful qualities that reside within all living beings. Regardless of the load of crap currently stuck to my sandals, the sweetness of the goats, the men in their ox carts, and the women bent over in the rice paddies are pictures that will remain with me forever. How far I have traveled from home, and how strange is the land I am in? I am reminded to appreciate the world and everything in it.

Anticipating a long, hot shower following my final jungle excursion, I stop at the outdoor bar for a soft drink, glance at the blackboard, and see my name beneath something called Elephant Wash. Elephant wash, huh? Where in my itinerary is Elephant Wash? I go up to the bartender and ask him, "What does this mean?"

He says, "Elephant wash."

"Yes, but what does it *mean*?"

The bartender repeats it with a verb thrown in: "Elephant gets washed."

"By whom?" I ask.

"By you," he says.

My jaw drops. "Me?"

"Yes. You ride, you wash."

I swallow my astonishment. Nixing the hot shower until later, I follow the guide down to the river, where I meet Mumbai once more. At least I think it's Mumbai, because how can you tell one elephant from another? I assume that washing the elephant means being handed a scrub brush and doing my best to wash a leg or two—or at least the lower half—but I'm instructed to get on top of that beast again. But this time I am given a choice. I can use a stool to mount her as she lies in the water or I can climb up her trunk as the guide demonstrates. The way my jungle experience has gone thus far, I opt for the stool. After numerous tries I am finally able to swing my leg up and over Mumbai's hulk. By the time she stands up, I am soaking wet and in a bareback straddle. I quickly find out it is a grave misnomer to call it an elephant wash. It should be called an Ellie wash as Mumbai proceeds to spray herself and me over and over again with her trunk. Sitting so high above the water, hanging on for dear life and sputtering like a wet seal, my overall concern is how to stay on the back of a wet, slippery elephant with little to grab or hold on to. Answer, you don't. I can't wait to get off. And get off I do, sliding right into the river.

Sliding down an elephant is definitely not the same as a waterslide. Drenched and muddy, I slowly make my way back to base camp. I approach the blackboard for the last time and erase my name. And that's how I spent the remainder of my last day in Paradise, getting washed by my new best friend, Mumbai the elephant. How many of you can say you have washed an Asian elephant in the depths of the Nepali jungle? More to the point, how many of you can say you were bathed by an elephant?

It's evening, and I'm repacking Big Red again. I stare at way too many things and pull out the unused Waterpik and the half gallon of Permethrin, knowing it's time to unload more stuff. I leave them both behind along with the now crappy sandals and the no longer pristine outfit I arrived in. My deployment list has grown from those college and camp t-shirts in Bhutan to the snacks I left on the trail for the invisible, exotic jungle creatures I never saw. Hopefully someone will find some use for the Permethrin and the partially used Deet spray. The Waterpik too, if someone can figure out how to use it. I'm not sure who would want the sandals, but I cleaned them up rather nicely with what was left of the liquid Woolite. When I am done rearranging Big Red, I zip and lift her. For the first time she is lighter, definitely lighter. I look back at my parting gifts. Will this be enough? Am I actually starting to let go? Not by a long shot.

I'm rather hard-pressed to agree that I've had the best possible wildlife experience. Through no fault of Asian Pacific Adventures, it was anything but predictable. But hasn't unpredictability been the theme since I left home? I do feel I experienced my own authentic approach to the jungle. I have, admittedly, been physically and emotionally weighed down by my ridiculous attempts to keep up my rituals and my mostly unused or useless must-haves—all the inappropriate stuff that almost equaled my own weight. By the time I leave, I realize that all I really needed was a backpack with the true essentials plus jeans, several t-shirts, and real sneakers for my entire trip. Each time I open and close Big Red or have to drag her through an airport, the Universe sends me Red alerts. In a real sense she is an expression of who I am: an attachment to stuff and a compulsive need to have my life perfectly planned and put together. I am finding that my stuff not only takes up suitcase space and requires the largest piece of luggage to be found, it takes up space in my mind, limiting me from experiencing the true purpose of my journey: finding a more simplistic and authentic lifestyle. Red's lesson, I believe, runs contrary to American Express. You *should* leave home without it.

As I drift off to sleep, I'm humming, "In the jungle, the mighty jungle, the lion sleeps tonight. Wimoweh, wimoweh, Wimoweh."

CHAPTER THIRTY-FOUR

Leaving the mighty jungle

May 19, Bharatpur airport, Nepal

Today, as I wait to be taken to the airport, the driver arrives with three new guests, an elderly man in a suit accompanied by two women wearing lovely dresses and sandals. I refrain from being judgmental about their attire considering how I arrived in the same Jeep wearing a white blouse and cream-colored capris. The older woman approaches me and asks whether I enjoyed my stay. Before I can answer, she confides that she hates the wilderness, heat, and bugs of all kind. She is only here because her husband and his sister both love safari experiences. She goes on to tell me they will be here for three days, which she hopes will be enough time to see the promised variety of exotic and endangered species. She wants to know what animals I've seen. I'm not sure how to answer. Should I tell her the whole truth and nothing but the truth, some half-truths, or a total lie? I can tell they aren't American, so I ask, "Have you ever seen crocodiles before?"

"No," she replies.

"Spotted deer?" Again she says no. I'm on a roll. "How about exotic butterflies?" A half-truth, I know. Excitedly, she says no. I reply, "Then you're in the right jungle."

She smiles and hurries off with her family to meet their guide for the Elephant Safari Ride before I have a chance to suggest a change of clothing. Oh, how I wish I could be a fly, or more appropriately a mosquito, on the wall during *their* safari!

The trip to the airport is in the same disgusting Jeep, along the same treacherous road, and it's just as hot as when I arrived. As we jostle and grind along, I think about my prissy attitude toward the resort's accommodations and its amenities. Did I really expect to bed down in a hotel with all the comforts of home in a jungle environment? Yes, believe it or not, I did. I got what I deserved: a plethora of creature comforts of the jungle kind, mosquitoes and other insects, geckos, and the sparsest of accommodations. But there's still hope for me. I've gotten a tad smarter over the last few days. I'm now wearing my dried-out jeans and t-shirt from the elephant wash, and I no longer give a rat's ass how grimy my jungle limousine is.

Waiting for my return flight to Niti's house, in preparation for my trip to Tibet, I'm not sure how to describe politely what is billed as the fourth busiest and one of the most prominent airports in Nepal. It looks like a building that's been untouched and uninhabited for years. It has one entrance for arrivals and one exit for departures. There is something to say for its simplicity. No need to run to catch your flight.

As I cast about for a clean seat, I spot a VIP sign on the door next to the arrival gate. The Hollywood clan perhaps? It seems impossible even to think there's a VIP room, but I regret not peeking inside.

I need to use the restroom but decide to eat my boxed lunch first. A middle-aged couple is sitting across from me. The woman is as white as a ghost, sweating profusely, and holding her abdomen. She looks awful. Over the course of the next thirty minutes her husband slowly and painstakingly walks her back and forth to the restroom, which houses one of those repulsive toilet pits. Each time she exits she looks worse than she did before she went in. At one point I think she might faint. It's not all that difficult to figure out what's ailing her: the traveler's nightmare, Montezuma's revenge. When she comes out from behind the cement enclosure after her most recent run to the toilet, she looks as if she wants to just crawl in a hole and die. Just not that hole.

I decide no matter how badly I have to go I will not follow in her footsteps. I'm sure the last thing this woman wants to do is get on a small prop plane with no bathroom. I empathize with her plight and can almost feel her desperation to end it all right here. With my eyes closed, I thank Buddha for protecting me this far from that fate. I pray she will feel better soon, and I make darned sure I add an addendum to my prayer. Please God, don't let her sit next to me on the plane.

Snapping back to reality, I hear our boarding announcement. That dreadful scene at the Frankfurt airport resurfaces. *Not this time*, I think, and hurry into line, pushing my way forward, determined not to be left behind.

On board, as that poor woman passes by, I settle in with my head back and realize that I can't let the whole bathroom thing and my compulsions about it define my *trip of a lifetime*. Not to mention all the unexpected things that have happened. This adventure is bigger than that. I'm convinced this is part of my lesson in letting go. Boy, are some things hard to overcome.

CHAPTER THIRTY-FIVE

The roof of the world and swine flu

May 20, Lhasa, Tibet

Today I'm heading to Tibet, the roof of the world. As I prepare to leave for the ancient capital of Lhasa—the highest city in the world at 12,000 feet—altitude sickness is on my mind. I experienced some problems while visiting Tiger's Nest Monastery, and that was only 10,000 feet. To be sure I would remember to take the Diamox twenty-four hours before departure, I slapped sticky notes around my room. Of course, one wasn't enough!

It's time to check in for my flight, and I'm sick of dragging and/or pushing Big Red. Clearly she's still too heavy despite my recent purge. I know more must go, but what?

I've been in Asia for two weeks now, but this will be my first opportunity to see Mount Everest up close. The sky is crystal clear, perfect for viewing the Himalayas—the kings of the world. The border between Tibet and Nepal runs right through the peak of Everest. Our pilot promises to let us know when it is almost in view. Peering out the window, I look down at the towering, snow-capped mountains as the clouds float below the peaks.

The pilot makes his announcement and of course, I'm on the wrong side of the plane. I jump out of my seat and into an empty one across the aisle, next to an older Chinese gentleman.

He is kind enough to let me lean over him while I snap photos of the Himalayan vistas. Everest literally takes my breath away and brings tears to my eyes. The passengers are silent except for the occasional *ah*. My trip could end tomorrow and still be complete in every way.

It was a short flight, and our landing in Lhasa is uneventful. That is, until a team of gowned and masked medical personnel swarm on board. The swine flu has reached China. We aren't going anywhere. All I can think is, *Damn, I can't catch a break.*

Two hours pass and we are still on the plane while the medical personnel take everyone's temperature. As I wait my turn, I wonder what the odds are of me having a temperature and decide not to leave it to chance. My seat is in the back of the plane near the bathroom. I duck in, hurriedly wet some paper towels with cold water, and slither back into my seat, tucking them inside my blouse under my armpits. As the thermometer-wielding, masked official approaches, I take out the towels, toss them under my seat, and pray. I have no idea what my Chinese seatmate is thinking as he watches my antics, but the end result is a normal temperature. Unfortunately, several people have higher-than-normal temperatures, so we aren't released until they all have retakes.

Thinking the coast is clear, we deplane and walk to the baggage claim area, where I overhear someone say we will now have to line up in the terminal and continue to wait while the individuals who have temperatures are pulled out of the line and sent for further testing. I catch a glimpse of what looks like a scene from a disaster movie. A handful of passengers are pulled from our line. The rest of us can continue on our way, but only as far as the door. We will now wait another two hours until they determine if those held back are sick enough to be sent to the hospital. This means that anyone seated near them will be taken to the hospital as well, just in case they've been infected. My Chinese gentleman friend is not among those retained, so I'm okay, but we still have to wait for all the results to come in. I practice detachment and deep breathing, but my Western impatience persists.

Today will be spent acclimating to the high altitude. I have been instructed by my travel agent to move slowly and rest often. I wonder what could possibly be slower than sitting on the airport floor for hours. I fill my time wondering whether my guide will be as attentive and interesting as Yeshey and Keshar. Will it be quiet and serene here like Bhutan or noisy and chaotic like Nepal? Will the Tibetan people be as warm and friendly? My thoughts wander to Tibetan cuisine. My appetite has come back full force, and I'm ready to try everything. Finally, we are allowed to leave the terminal.

After hours of sitting and standing, I spot my guide Sherab's sign with a mix of exhaustion and relief.

CHAPTER THIRTY-SIX

Food for thought

May 21, Tsedang Hotel, Tibet

Sherab, who looks to be in his late twenties, greets me by placing a lovely white, silk scarf called a *khata* around my neck, a gesture of welcome. On the two-hour drive to Tsedang, located at the foot of Mount Gongbori, we travel alongside the Yarlong Tsangpo River. More than 700 miles long, it originates from a glacier in the Himalayas and runs through the heart of Tibet before making an abrupt hairpin turn straight to India. Called the Everest of Rivers by adventure seekers, parts of the river have never been explored and are considered dangerous.

Luck has been on my side in the weather department at least, with sunny skies ever since I arrived in Asia. With the clear, still waters of the Tsango River on my left and miles of forests mixed with flowering bushes, wildflowers, and the stunning Himalayas to my right, I settle in and enjoy the ride.

I did have one pressing question: the state of the bathroom facilities. Sherab explained that the Western toilet is making inroads into China in the big cities and the airports. Since that's not where we will be spending our time, I will once again be faced with squatty potties or the great outdoors. Will I be able to maintain my hold out? I may have to resume the chicken broth, toast, and tea for practical reasons. Time, along with my food choices, will tell.

The hotel in Tsedang is stunning, the best hotel so far. I'm pretty tired, so I beg off going out to dinner and opt for room service. Even though my appetite is back I order soup, toast, and black tea, saving Tibetan food for tomorrow. My tray is brought up by two young Asian women. Noticing the only utensils are a set of chopsticks, I request a spoon, but they don't understand English so I wave the chopsticks in the air while shaking my head no. Nodding, they leave the room. One of them comes right back with another set of chopsticks. Obviously, something got lost in the translation. Too tired to perform another round of charades, I slurp the broth from the bowl. I will discover utensils are not always a necessity.

The next morning there's quite a variety on the breakfast buffet, including something very American: Rice Krispies and milk. There's nothing like a little snap, crackle, and pop to start your morning, music to my ears. I'm not alone in my choice.

A stately gentleman, impeccably dressed in an expensive suit, sits across from me. I try not to stare at him despite being captivated by his large bowl filled with *zanba*, a dough made of barley flour, yak butter, and water, a staple food in Tibet. I watch as he puts some *ghee* (unsalted butter) into the bowl and pours in some boiling water. He rotates the bowl, mixing it with his right hand, using no utensils. He proceeds to knead the mixture into small dough balls, squeezing each one into his mouth. Watching him is like watching the Food Network back home, but without any forks, knives, or spoons. I'm told Tibetans believe eating with your hands is better for digestion.

The dinner menu was posted in the elevator and featured fungus in yak bones, chicken and caterpillar, stewed Tibet sheep's head, and bird's nest soup, along with sea cucumber, fish bladder, and pork uterus. I stopped reading after pickles and penis. When Sherab asks if I want to eat dinner here, I politely say no. I tell him we need to find a more Americanized version of Chinese food, like a good ol' pu pu platter.

Over the next several days I learn more about the local cuisine. Here are just a few to wet or ruin your appetite: Bird's nest soup is made from the nests of tiny birds called swiflets. The nests are made from their saliva. When it is exposed to the air, it hardens into dried spit. Everything is removed, and the nest is soaked for several days. When it falls apart, it leaves behind thin, clear, gooey noodles that can be served as dinner or dessert.

The sea cucumber comes from the ocean and resembles a spiky gherkin pickle. After it has been soaked in water, it expands to the size of a dill pickle and has a jelly-like texture. I'm told it has no taste, so why bother? If you want to get close to an American dish, there is Tibetan pizza, but you won't see pepperoni or sausage on it. Tibetan toppings include, but are not limited to, yak meat, pig fat, melon, and morsels of wood-ear fungus. Look it up if you like. If all the above doesn't start your stomach churning, get this. Penises turn up in many hot dishes. They come from a wide variety of animals: yaks, cows, horses, donkeys, dogs, lambs, and snakes. They are all considered good for your bones, muscles, kidneys, blood circulation, and for clearing your lungs. Women get an added benefit. The high protein content is said to be good for their skin. I'll pass on all fronts.

I've learned a lot about this topic, so hang on. When animal penises are prepared, some are cut lengthwise while others are sliced into round rings, like calamari. They are usually accompanied by dishes of sesame, soy, and chili sauces for dipping. The most coveted and expensive part of the penis is the root, which is darker, softer in texture, and more nutritious. Is your mouth watering yet? Each animal's penis has a different taste and texture. A deer penis is flaccid and tastes salty. The lamb's is crunchy and like munching on beef tendon. A cow penis is fatter, chewier, and has more flavor compared with a sheep penis, which is hard. And what about that snake penis? Well, a snake is blessed with two penises. You get twice the bang for your yuan, but you might feel shortchanged by their size.

There are even penis restaurants in China. One in particular recommends the hot pot for beginners, which offers a sampling of six types of penis and four types of testicle. Ready to book your reservation? Finally, you must cook penis properly because then it's soft, has little flavor, and is easy to swallow with little chewing needed. That sounds convenient if you can get past the mental aspects of it. My thoughts? I'll take my chances with an Oscar Mayer wiener. What it lacks in health benefits, it makes up for in flavor.

The irony is that in Bhutan the human penis is revered. They pay homage to it in a variety of art forms whereas China and Tibet place great importance on consuming the animal variety. One man's delicacy is another man's belief, I guess. As for me, my adventurous spirit in the food category has disappeared.

CHAPTER THIRTY-SEVEN

The road less traveled

"There ain't no surer way to find out whether you like people or hate them than to travel with them."
~ Mark Twain

May 22, Samye Monastery, Tsedang, Tibet

This morning we will visit Tibet's first monastery, Samye. A destination for Buddhist pilgrims, they will walk thousands of miles to get here. Surrounded by a massive stone wall topped by 108 tiny chortens, the monastery has the typical ornate roofline, and colorful walls. The main temple represents the mythical mountain Meru. Ancient Buddhists believed the universe was flat and that Meru was at the center.

The thick, acrid scent of incense in a massive stone burner located in the courtyard makes my eyes water. The pilgrims wear different combinations of bright colors that identify which part of Tibet they are from. As I admire the women, I notice they seem just as interested in me. Perhaps they think my brightly colored sundress is symbolic of my overdressed tribe. The locals who come here wear jeans and jackets. As in Bhutan and Nepal, the West has reached them. Circumambulating clockwise around the large stone wall, they turn their handheld prayer wheels or finger their mala beads, chanting and praying for blessings. Along the route are rows of large prayer wheels waiting to be gently turned, sending prayers to the heavens. It feels like I'm back at the King's Memorial Chorten in Bhutan and makes me miss Yeshey.

Outside the main temple are a pair of spectacular stone lions, two exquisite, white marble elephants, and a three-foot-wide bronze bell that hangs on a cross beam. Called the Three Style-Temple, the first floor is Tibetan, the second Chinese, and the third Hindu. Here you do not have to take off your hat or your shoes as you enter, but once inside it will cost you five dollars to take photos—well worth the price.

The Tibetan floor is dominated by an assembly hall full of religious murals, statues, and important relics, many enclosed in glass. In spite of the high ceilings, the room is almost dark save for the flickering butter candles. I can make out elaborate images of the Buddha in the murals on the walls and various tapestries hanging from the ceiling. Excited, we see one of Tibet's most important sacred images, a two-dimensional sand mandala several feet long and several feet wide, it is mounted on a table and protected under glass. Mandalas are geometric figures that use Hindu and Buddhist symbols to depict the universe and are used as an aid during meditation. Constructing these large mandalas

is labor-intensive and can take days or weeks to complete. Several monks will work together, each assigned to a specific area. The design is constructed from the center out and is incredibly intricate. This mandala required a week of eighteen-hour days to create and ultimately will be destroyed during a ceremony by a high-ranking lama. The sand will be collected and poured into a nearby river to release its positive energy. Its destruction represents the central Buddhist teaching of the impermanence of all things. In the West, we struggle with this key tenet of

Buddhism. How much happier our existence would be if we could accept that permanence is a myth.

The monks sit on mats in neat rows facing each other. One monk leads the prayer and chants from the ancient scriptures. Their low-pitched voices vibrate through the hall. Letting go, I listen, mesmerized. A sudden clang of a gong triggers a musical symphony, with several monks beating large, double-sided drums with their curved drumsticks while others blow through conch shells. There are breaks in the praying and chanting when two monks play fifteen-foot-long horns called *dungchens*. The most widely used instrument in Tibetan Buddhist culture, dungchens have been compared to the singing of elephants.

We listen for a while, then enter a small temple. Considered the artistic highlight of Samye, it houses a statue of a male with 1,000 arms. Each hand has a perfectly painted eye on it. It's called the *bodhisattva*—an enlightened being—of compassion.

To the right of the assembly hall we enter a protector chapel with eerie statues of demons who were turned into Buddhist protector deities. Frightening to look at, I wouldn't want to wake up to one staring down at me. Passing through three tall, painted doorways we come to a chapel where a twelve-foot statue of Buddha is enshrined. Before heading upstairs, we stop to view a large, golden Buddha draped with offerings of white scarves. The size and beauty of this statue render me speechless.

The second floor is Chinese and has an open roof area where monks and locals are crafting artwork for the temples. One chapel houses a head-spinning number of stone Buddhas. We walk out onto a porch to inspect a thirty-foot mural called the *Painted Historical Records*, which depicts the religious history of Tibet.

On the third floor we encounter the rooms the Dalai Lama used when he visited Samye. There's a small anteroom, throne room, and a bedroom with a glass case holding relics. Sherab points to some hair, a walking stick, and a skull—relics from two of the founders of Samye—and a Tara statue that is said to speak. Normally, there are so many people crammed into this room that it's impossible to stay for long, but the crowd must have dissipated.

This floor has little to see except for the wonderful views surrounding the monastery and an inner chapel where a long line of visitors is waiting to enter. I understand why when I spot the sign on the door: CHAPEL OF LONGEVITY. Back home this line would likely resemble the mob scene outside Walmart on Black Friday. One line represents health and well-being. The other? Not so much.

Following the pilgrims in front, and gently shoved by those behind me, I enter. The room houses every Buddha image known to man. The energy here encourages me to say a silent prayer for a long and healthy life.

Exploring the temple, I come upon a number of altars adorned with religious objects and intricate cakes made of butter. They are sculpted by Tibetan monks into beautiful flowers, animals, and other Buddhist symbols.

Back on the first floor we once again pass through the assembly hall where a Tibetan ceremony is now being held. Total silence fills the room, and we come upon the stunning sight of two rows of monks facing each other with their heads bowed. I assume they are in deep prayer, because not one is stirring. Walking closer, I do a double take when I discover that these are empty robes. Each one has been perfectly draped and formed into the shape of a hooded monk in prayer position. I forgot to ask if this has a special spiritual meaning or is simply a stylistic display.

The number of statues of different Buddhas in various poses has a dizzying affect. Common in every temple I've visited in all three kingdoms, the poses, called *mudras*, all symbolize different facets of the Buddha. In some cases, the Buddha is in the seated lotus position with his hands relaxed in his lap and the tips of his thumbs and fingers touching each other, representing a meditative state. In other renditions, the Buddha is seated with his left hand in his lap and his right hand raised, representing the teachings of the Dharma. I like this position because it symbolizes enlightenment not only for him, but for all sentient beings. If only that's all you needed to do to become enlightened: left hand in lap, right hand in air.

I feel a headache starting, the likely cause, all the details, images, and history coming at me from every direction. I've absorbed perhaps a tenth of what is meaningful and important.

I'm disappointed that we won't be visiting any villages; but here they are made up of only a dozen or so houses each, and all are miles from the nearest roads. The people lead simple lives farming and tending sheep. Many homes have no electricity, plumbing, or running water; and the inhabitants have never seen a TV, airplane, or tourists.

While we're discussing Tibetan life, I mention to Sherab the Bhutanese method for protecting their homes. He's familiar with it and says that the Tibetan is a bit unusual. Although I can't imagine anything stranger than the Divine Mad Monk's thunderbolt, he tells me how Tibetans make balls of sacred rice mixed with cow dung and place them over their doorways. The thunderbolt is gaining more appeal by the minute.

As in Bhutan and Nepal, life here is dominated by prayer and each tiny home has a prayer room. One bit of information is not lost on me: Tibetans don't have bathrooms or pit toilets. They squat outside wherever and whenever and never worry about anyone seeing them. Am I in trouble here?

We will take a different route back to Lhasa, one with better photo opportunities. The alternate route is over 160 miles along the world's highest plateau and at 16,000 feet, gives way to the Yarlung River, the highest river in the world, which flows into the world's deepest canyon: the Yarlung Zangbo Grand Canyon. Spectacular I'm sure, but right now only one thing registers: 160 miles and *no toilet!* Yes, I'm in trouble, *big* trouble! I try to block out this information. I take a deep breath, lean back, and try to enjoy the ride as I utter a fervent prayer: "Please Lord, let this be a smooth ride, and let me hold it in the whole way, please!"

Fields of colorful prayer flags rise from the bleached, rolling dunes and rear up against the backdrop of the green Himalayas and their snow-covered peaks. It puts me in a peaceful frame of mind, but not for long. Not well-suited for the faint of heart, this trip soon proves to be the route from hell.

The heat is stifling. The road is a track of massive bumps, hills, and rocks, unleashing clouds of dust and dirt. Without air-conditioning, you have to leave the windows open and inhale nasty plumes of the stuff. I could use one of those Kathmandu masks at this point. I decide to keep the windows closed and put up with the heat. I'm confident that I can tolerate two hours of heat—the length of time it took to get here from Lhasa. After all, nothing could be as bad as those jungle Jeep rides in Nepal.

The first two hours pass, and I'm informed it may take several more. I'm so overheated and fed up that I begin asking in my best frustrated child voice, "How much longer?"

Sherab's good-natured answer for everything remains "No worries." I'm starting to hate that phrase. He proceeds to tell me how far in meters. I have to keep reminding him I want to know how *long* in time. I am getting hotter, and more impatient, by the minute. This vehicle feels like a violent bouncing machine under my butt. Once more, in yet another kingdom, my body is taking a beating. Up ahead, I spot what I think is a real paved road, but it's a mirage.

Now I know why the "inflatable pillow, excellent for long drives" was on the travel agency's list of stuff to bring, which of course I didn't. I also remember reading "the roads in Tibet are rough and dusty, and travel will be rugged, but you will have had a chance to visit the world's most seductive destinations, so enjoy your journey to the *Lost Horizon*." Sorry, I don't feel the least bit seduced. And those memorable lines, "The spectacular scenery is well worth the uncomfortable rides. These are rare roses, which crown the thorny stem." Really?

It gets so bad that I find myself emitting an audible "*Jesus Fucking Christ*." Sherab turns and asks what I'm saying. I tell him it's an American version of a blessing. Again, Buddhism seems out of reach. *Oh Mary, Mother of God*, I think. *If I keep this up, I'll go straight to hell in a handbasket.* Catholic girl strikes again!

As we rock along, I tap Sherab on the back and tell him that not only am I hot, tired, and sweaty, I'm hungry.

He replies, "We will stop when I find a tree to sit under and eat our box lunches." When he adds, "No worries," I open my mouth to say something caustic, then think better of it.

I haven't seen a tree for miles, and if he doesn't find one soon, I'm going to bite his head off. Fortunately for him, we come upon two trees, one on the side of the road and another a short distance away. That's the one where I will stake my claim to fame, but not before we eat.

I open my box lunch and find no utensils or napkins. Hungrily, I shove the food into my mouth and, since I am already sweaty and dirty, what do I use as a napkin to wipe my mouth? The bottom hem of my once clean, perky sundress. Yes, you heard right. Perhaps you know me well enough by now to know this is the last thing Ellie Dias would ever be caught doing, let alone in public. But I'm nearing the end of my *trip of a lifetime*, and I no longer care. Nor do I give a damn about how unkempt I feel, with greasy, limp hair and streaked makeup.

My belly is full, and so is my bladder. Unsure how much longer we still have to go or how many rocks and bumps lie in wait ahead, I glance at the tree in the distance. Knowing *full* well I can't hold it any longer even under the best of circumstances, I make the only choice there is. I hurry over to the tree and pick the side that will provide me with the most coverage. Sherab and our driver have their backs to me as they finish their lunches. Except for a shepherd and his pack of sheep coming round the bend, it looks as if I can stay fairly hidden if I can be quick. Nervously, I plant my feet firmly on the ground and, with nothing to hold on to, pull down my underwear and do the squat. Nothing happens. Nervous out here in the great outdoors, I tell myself to relax and take a few deep breaths. Ahh, blessed relief at last. Emerson and Thoreau would be proud. Just me, the bees, and the butterflies communing with nature. A couple of stray sheep wander over and decide to join in with a welcomed "Ba-a-a-ah" and let loose right beside me. This must be a magic spot. I admit, this open-air site under the tree beats the heck out of those pit toilets. At least here you can breathe while executing the deed.

It dawns on me that I can't remain in this position, communing with Mother Nature, for much longer. The herder will catch up with his sheep, and I'll be literally caught with my pants down.

Elimination in the great outdoors may seem small and insignificant to some, but for me it is anything but. Maybe taking this alternative route was meant to be. It has offered me the chance not only to experience the physical release of "letting go" in a bodily function, but to experience a mental release as well. For the first time, going all the way back to my announcement "I'm going to the Himalayas," I don't have to plot or plan or think my way through things. I feel as if I'm dropping more than just my pants; I'm dropping my precious ego as well.

Back in the car, as we continue to jerk along, a nomad coming down from the hills waves his hand at us. I wave back, thinking it is just a friendly gesture. Nope. The driver stops and asks if it's okay if we give this stranger a ride. He has lost his yak and is looking for it. Not part of the package deal, I think, but what can I say? Besides, I figure I need to make up for the bad karma I've been creating with my attitude. "Sure, why not?" I say, half under my breath. This whole experience can't get much more bizarre, so I might as well just let go, again!

The nomad tries to squeeze into the front seat with the driver and Sherab, but I really want to redeem myself in Buddha's eyes, so I suggest he sit next to me. Every time I spot a yak I touch the nomad on his shoulder and say, "Look, over there, over there." I'm beginning to sound like my jungle guide. Finally, a fair distance from where we picked him up, he asks the driver to let him out. He walks up the hill, passing a yak on the way. Not his, I guess.

What I remember from my reading is that nomads live in groups of ten to twenty-five families. Most live in tents made from black yak hair or wool and are held up by wooden poles. I ask if we can stop and look inside one. I'm curious about how nomads live and desperate to take a break. We drive over to one of the tents, and Sherab asks permission for us to go inside. The nomad greets us warmly, and we follow him into his tent. I notice he has a picture of the Dalai Lama around his neck, and several strings of prayer beads. He shows us his surroundings and invites us to sit on the floor with his family, and offers me a cup of butter tea. I panic, knowing how bad it tastes until I remember what I learned from Yeshey: don't empty your cup unless you want a refill. I give silent thanks to him.

As I pretend to sip my tea, my eyes light on an altar dedicated to various Buddhist deities. There is a cooking stove, sheepskin sleeping mats, and yak-hair blankets. They use the open hearth in the middle of the tent to make a fire from yak dung to keep them warm. The average family can have up to fifty yaks, so they never run out of fuel or the materials to make those protection balls. The tents are easy to dismantle and move, which is perfect for a herdsman's life. Along the route today, I've also noticed cave dwellings built into the hillsides. At four feet wide and six feet tall, you'd better like your relatives, a lot!

Stepping outside, I spot a blanket of brown stuff spread out in the sun. One whiff and I know it's yak dung. The women go out each morning to collect and spread it out to dry. It's an important chore since all the cooking and heating depend on this dried dung. I think of that motley crew of dogs back home and laugh. I can relate to the chore of having to pick up dung on one too many occasions. At least I didn't have to dry it out too.

As we get back in the car, I ask why the people here are so dirty. Their faces, hands, and clothes are caked with mud; even their hair is matted. There is little water to wash with on this high plateau, but the nomads also consider washing to be unhealthy, I'm told. When they do wash, it is by rinsing their face and hands in yak or goat milk. Some of them go their entire life without ever taking a bath. This explains why the nomad we picked up smelled so bad. I ask about the picture of the Dalai Lama around the nomad's neck, considering the disdain the government has for him. Sherab says that Tibetans are still loyal to him but must do so in secret because if caught they could go to jail. I wonder if I will live long enough to see a world in which people are not persecuted for their beliefs.

Back in the sweat box again, we pass nomads—their tents surrounded by prayer flags—doing their chores. Yaks roam in the distance. These few stops to observe and take photos are the only saving grace of this long, hot, dusty ride and ease my irritation for a while. When I see an actual highway up ahead,

I want to kiss the ground. We are back in Lhasa.

Entering the hotel, I'm weary and achy, which reminds me of what Buddha once said: "It is better to travel well than to arrive." I'll remember that, but for now I prefer Jerry Seinfeld's "Sometimes the road less traveled is less traveled for a reason."

CHAPTER THIRTY-EIGHT

What is the sound of one hand clapping?

May 22, ancient Sera Thekchenling Monastery, Lhasa

Even though I took Diamox before leaving Kathmandu, I've been having daily headaches that are probably altitude related. I'm running out of meds for migraines, yet I still have a ton of vitamins left. Most days I completely forget to take them.

After checking into the Kyichu Tibetan Style Hotel, we head off to the ancient Sera Thekchenling Monastery. Situated on 28 acres, this is one of the three great monasteries of Tibet. It's not a place of worship, but a monastic university that provides religious education to monks until age seventy. At one time, more than 5,000 monks studied here.

The whitewashed monastery stands at the end of a long, narrow road. Walking up the steep steps, we pass several buildings on either side. In the center of the monastery are the ruins of what was likely once a temple. I'm given no further explanation. Tibetans say little against the Chinese government. I stare at the rubble, remembering what I had read. More than 6,000 monasteries and temples housing priceless jewels, Thangka paintings, and valuable documents were destroyed by the Chinese army. Only a handful remain. Despite the Occupation, the Buddhists' faith did not fade, and they have held fast to their traditions, culture, and Buddhism. I have seen this firsthand since I arrived and marvel at the strength of their spirit in the face of horrific adversity.

We come to a set of red double doors with a sign overhead: DEBATING COURTYARD. The monastery is famous for the debates held in this enclosed yard every day at three o'clock. Inside, I encounter red-robed monks, both young and old, sitting in small groups under the trees and practicing traditional Tibetan debating. Rather like sparring matches, a senior monk stands up in front of a group of junior monks and fires off questions accentuated by hand gestures.

The purpose is to keep the young monks focused on Buddhist doctrine and philosophical concepts. During the debates they study a philosophical point and try to establish its validity through reasoning, and I have a front-row seat. Even though I can't understand their lively exchanges, it's fascinating to observe the monks' debating choreography and expressive faces. With graceful movements, the senior monks drive their point home by rocking forward, lifting one leg, slapping their hands, and snapping their mala beads at the seated monks. These gestures force the seated monks to jerk back when the mala beads get too close to their faces as the senior monk pushes them for an answer. Although serious in nature, the courtyard is filled with laughter, energy, and enthusiasm. I want to be reincarnated as a monk teaching philosophy. I can see myself standing up in front of my class, posing a question, slapping my hands, and snapping my beads.

After the debate is over, I sit outside the courtyard and wait for Sherab to return from who knows where. I ask a local to explain more about the debating process. It can be either a Buddhist scripture or something like the example he gives me: "You are facing a house that has just been built. After you walk through the door, is it still a new house or is it an old house?"

After the monk presents the question, he clasps his left palm with his right hand and pulls the left hand backward. Each gesture has a specific meaning. The right hand pushing down in a clapping motion signifies a wrong answer, and the left hand raised in the clapping motion symbolizes a correct answer. Known as *koans*, these puzzles can be presented as a story, a question, or a statement. The meaning can't be understood by rational thinking. Koans help one go beyond the thinking mind. Most people are familiar with the koan: two hands clap and there is a sound; what is the sound of one hand clapping?

I ask about the monks and their training since the Chinese occupation. I did a little reading about Sera before I left the States and recall that monks are no longer allowed to enter the monastery at the age of eight but must wait until they are sixteen, and they can no longer study Tibetan Buddhism in the depth that previous generations did.

He answers evasively and, like my guide, does not offer any information about the impact the invasion has had on the Tibetan people, physically and spiritually. If I want to know more, I will have to research this on my own.

Sherab returns and takes me to a building where locals do woodblock printing. The walls are lined with rows and rows of red-painted shelves, many filled with darkened, wooden blocks carved with scriptures.

Some shelves contain modern books along with stacks of long, slender pages of traditional scriptures. Stacks of them line the floor as well. I've seen these scriptures being read at most of the monasteries I've visited. I take a video of a Tibetan sitting on the floor, printing. With the paper on top of the block and using a hard pad and a rubbing technique, he chants and prays aloud. On my way out, I notice a bunch of black-printed good luck banners on yellow fabric and I buy one. Good-bye, thunderbolt and sacred rice dung balls!

I wait outside for Sherab and notice an eye chart tacked up on a piece of wood. Rather than just stand around waiting, I decide to test my eyes. Several Tibetans soon join me in a game of "who can see the best." In the good ol' USA, you have to pay for an eye exam; in Tibet it's free entertainment! Almost everything here is done outdoors. Do four walls and a door make a difference?

Sitting in a lovely garden outside my hotel room, I wait for my dinner of a grilled ham and cheese sandwich, pickle, and black tea. It's been my dinner for the last two nights. I decide that if I ever travel to a strange land again, I will save a lot of money by *not* signing up for the meal plan. There are quite a few tourists outside, but as usual, I'm the only one sitting alone. It doesn't really matter, because no one is engaging in conversation. Everyone is focused on their open laptops or other wireless devices. Frowning into their electronic screens is more like it. I open my laptop to update my travel blog. As I try to access the Internet, I begin to understand their facial expressions. We are all locked out. The young girl who brings me my dinner tells me that Internet censorship is strictly enforced by the government. Many of the social networks, such as blogs and Facebook, as well as certain search engines, are forbidden. I give silent thanks for the privilege of living in a free country.

I update my blog offline, which I learned to do during my stay in Nepal and its constant power outages. One of Niti's computer instructors showed me how to transfer my documents to my blog once I get Internet access again. I realize how important my blog and journals are, not just for my cyberspace fellow travelers, but as a detailed account of my experiences.

CHAPTER THIRTY-NINE

She giveth, and she taketh away—my run-in with
Chinese officials

May 23, Jokhang Temple, Lhasa

It's another beautiful day in the neighborhood as we head to Jokhang Temple. Known as the House of the Lord, it is the most revered religious structure in Tibet.

We set out on the Barkhor path—called the pilgrimage circuit—a walkway that encircles the temple. It is lined with stalls of jewelry, mala beads, colorful Tibetan clothes, and prayer flags. I get a kick out of seeing a watermelon displayed next to a set of false teeth. Something for everyone, I guess.

Along the path we pass groups of monks sitting cross-legged on the ground uttering mantras, their alms bowls next to them. At first I think they're begging, but I'm told that alms bowls are common for wandering monks. They ask for nothing; they merely wait to receive an offering. Walking beside us are Tibetan nomads, both men and women, in their native dress. Most of the women wear their hair in braids; some have as many as 108, the Tibetan sacred number.

Because May is the most popular time for pilgrimages, there's a constant stream following the circular route, always traveling in a clockwise direction. Many move in a rhythmic motion. Fascinated, I watch as they touch their hands to their forehead, take a step forward, lower them in front of their face, take another step, lower them to their chest, bend down, place their hands on the ground and prostrate their body, touch the ground with their forehead, stand up, take three steps, and start over again, praying the entire way. Some are wearing rawhide knee pads and wooden planks attached to their hands for protection. Mixed into the steady hum and rhythm of their prayers, I hear the scraping of the wood along the stone pavement. Although they are covered in dust, dirt, and blood stains, I can't help but notice the blissful look on their faces as they step, bow, and bend. I struggle to put into words what it feels like watching this continuous stream of people slowly making their way to this sacred temple. You must see it to believe it.

Some of these pilgrims have been performing these prostrations for thousands of miles to reach a holy place like this. Even when they aren't making a pilgrimage, they are expected to prostrate themselves daily.

The Jokhang Temple is where monks will study Buddhist scriptures for the first time. They have other duties too, such as readying the temple for visitors by cleaning and filling the hundreds of butter lamps. By order of the Chinese government, only one hundred monks can stay here at any given time.

With its beautiful golden roof, the temple is four stories tall and covers about 75,000 square feet. It houses the sacred statue of the eighth-century Buddha, a twelve-year-old known as the Jowo Rinpoche. Enshrined within the temple walls, it is the holiest statue in Tibet. Also housed here are hundreds of sculptures, painted scrolls, and statues hidden away and inaccessible to tourists.

Two tall poles covered in prayer flags stand in the open area. Incense burning in two enormous pot-bellied burners fills the air. The area in front is filled with pilgrims prostrating and circumambulating the temple. The pilgrims are so focused they hardly notice as I carefully step between them, videotaping their faith in motion. Large red and gold prayer wheels are spun by the pilgrims as they chant their prayers. I join them, walking and spinning while silently giving thanks for being allowed to witness these holy rituals. Tibetan Buddhists believe they must recite or chant Buddhist scriptures many times during the day. Those who don't know them by heart can still offer them to the universe by turning the prayer wheels that house the scriptures inside.

Outside the massive, locked doors to the sanctuary, crowds

of pilgrims and tourists jostle for position. Once the doors are opened, I squeeze in along with everyone else. I'm hit with a cloud of incense; the scent is overpowering. The temple—a maze of chapels dedicated to various gods and bodhisattvas—is dark except for the endless rows of glowing red and gold butter lamps. Everything seems to be painted red: the floors, rafters, and pillars. Even the paintings and wall hangings have red and gold threads. All I hear is the melody of mantras. Because I am unable to understand them, Sherab tells me one is a prayer: May all sentient beings have happiness and avoid suffering—a prayer we all should consider daily.

Inside the middle of the temple is a small courtyard where I see the Dharma wheel—one of the oldest symbols in Buddhism—which represents Buddha's path to enlightenment. There are rows of benches covered with Tibetan rugs in the main temple. Here the monks will sit later in the evening as they chant prayers or scriptures. I join the long, single-file line of pilgrims and tourists that snakes around the temple walkways. We head deeper into the sanctuary. It's slow going as some of the pilgrims crawl on their hands and knees or continually prostrate as they make their way to the central shrine of Jowo Rinpoche. For the pilgrims, just seeing the statue means having a dialogue with Buddha. Elaborately carved and studded with gems, he is surrounded by large butter lamps. I follow the pilgrims' lead and touch my head to Jowo's knee while saying a simple prayer of appreciation and gratitude for all that I have in my life. Reflecting on how this spiritual act of paying homage to their most sacred icon is available to all regardless of their beliefs reminds me how the religion in which I was raised forbids many from receiving the extraordinary gift of the Eucharist.

I watch pilgrims carrying large plastic bags of yak butter. As they pass the chapels, they spoon butter into the lamps to keep the flames alive, another symbol of enlightenment. The monks diligently watch the lamps since many monasteries have been damaged by fire. I notice a lot of the pilgrims carry white scarves like the one I received on my arrival. They drape them on the statues or leaving them on the altars as a sign of respect and gratitude. People throw yuans of all denominations everywhere—on the altars and at the edges of walkways—along with grains of barley. They do this to gain merit or good karma that is carried over later in life or to a person's next life. Offerings are a central part of this culture, and Tibetans give without reservation. They may not have a pot to pee in, but they freely offer money and other goods.

After we explore the temple, we climb the stairs to the roof to see the unbelievable views of the Barkhor path and the nearby Potala Palace. Monks often debate on the roof in the late afternoon. Several elder monks sit down to tea, and one offers me a cup. Having a few moments to sit quietly, I once again find myself thinking about the churches back home, with their sparkling stained glass windows and shiny waxed floors. There the walls are painted in muted tones, giving them a light, airy feel. A stark contrast to the dark Tibetan temples illuminated only by butter lamps. Painted in bold reds, greens, and blues, the walls and doors are warped and crooked with age. The musty smell, dust, and cobwebs add to the ornate designs within their walls. Despite my obsessive-compulsive need for cleanliness, I'm more comfortable and at peace inside these temples. It must be the energy and the cumulative devotion, love, and intention emanating from the hearts of the Tibetan people.

Brought back to the present, I think how much I want to have my picture taken with these monks. As we are about to leave, I feel I can't miss this once-in-a-lifetime opportunity, so I

ask my guide to make my request. Delighted, they grin from ear
to ear as they crowd around me and want to see the picture right
away. They let out a string of hearty laughs when I show it to
them, giving me a thumbs up. Smiling, we bow to one another.

Back at the hotel, my headache returns. Just as I am about to lie
down, the front desk calls. There are some Chinese authorities
in the lobby who want to speak with me. What? I'm guilty of a
lot of stupid moves on this trip, but nothing to warrant being
sought by Chinese officials. Heading to the lobby, I wonder if
someone reported my underarm-cooling tactic on the plane.

   A uniformed man and a woman dressed in a suit introduce
themselves. My heart racing, I confirm that I am Ellie Dias.
The man begins to interrogate me about a recent banking
transaction I made that had culminated in a confusing mess.
Sherab had taken me to a local bank, where I tried to exchange
some traveler's checks for one hundred US dollars and one
hundred Chinese yuan. The confused teller kept going back and
forth from the counter to somewhere in the back of the bank.
Standing there waiting, I had no idea what was happening.
When she finally approached with my money, she counted it
several times, five to be exact. By the time we left the bank,

even Sherab was shaking his head.

The interrogator tells me in a serious tone that the woman in the suit, the bank teller, claims she gave me one hundred additional US dollars by mistake, and the authorities want it back. I give him a fixed stare. Not one to just hand over a hundred dollars without any proof, I begin a heated debate with them as visitors and hotel staff watch this absurd scenario. Insisting that there is no way she gave me an extra one hundred US dollars, I loudly inform them that I know how to count American dollars, though maybe not yuan. Like a tennis match we go back and forth, them claiming this, me claiming that. Because I am so adamant, they finally say it must have been the yuan that was the extra hundred. Since I've already used some of it, they ask me to sit with a pen and paper and try to remember everything I've spent the last two days. How crazy is this? By my calculations, it appears that the teller did made a mistake and gave me too many yuan, so I return the extra money. My irritation is tempered when I see that she is in quite a bit of trouble. Digging into my purse, I hand over the money. *Unbelievable.*

Heading back to my room to prepare for my next tour, I feel as if I'm in a scene from *1984,* where Big Brother has been watching me. By now my headache is a full-blown migraine. My *trip of a lifetime* is drawing to a close, and I hope these stranger-than-fiction scenarios are as well.

CHAPTER FORTY

Number nine, please! A great combo—a menu with a
diagnosis

May 23, Tibetan Medicine Hospital, Lhasa

Our next stop is a tour of the Tibetan Medicine Factory, which is part of the Herbal Medicine Hospital in Lhasa where illnesses are diagnosed using traditional methods.

Joining a small group, we are greeted by a doctor in a white lab coat and scrub cap who gives a short presentation on the 4,000-year-old history of medicine. He points to numerous thangkas that contain all aspects of medicine from its beginning to treatment methods such as herbal, acupuncture, and surgical procedures. Many of the scrolls show the anatomy of the human body and are used as teaching tools. I can't help but compare them to the texts I use to teach back home. Tibetan medicine has a close relationship to the Tibetan calendar and astronomy, and doctors here believe the body changes with the seasons. Much of what he tells us requires some additional reading to garner a better understanding. What registers loud and clear is that their approach is based on the belief that people get sick when their physical, psychological, and spiritual well-being are out of balance. If one part of the body is ailing, it all is. Even though it's becoming a popular form of holistic medicine in the US, many doctors still focus on the treatment of the symptoms rather than the person.

The factory produces an array of medicines used to treat hypertension, heart disease, paralysis, gastric ulcers, diabetes, kidney stones, and sexual dysfunction. He finishes by telling us that most common treatments are pills processed from herbs harvested in the Himalayas. They produce more than 160 different herb pills. I wonder what these Tibetan docs would think of my traveling pharmacy.

The tour ends with an opportunity to have a consultation with one of their physicians. When it's my turn, I ask him about my migraines. First, he studies my palms. I'm hoping he finds a long lifeline, because I feel half dead. Then he turns over my hands to look at my fingernails. He has me stick out my tongue, checks it, then looks at the whites of my eyes. Finally, he checks my pulse on both wrists—the primary method for their diagnosis. He asks how long I've had migraines. I tell him forty-three years.

"Oh no, forty-three years, must get chief doctor," he replies somberly.

Oh boy, I think, not just a second opinion—no prior approval or formal referral here—I'm going to see the head honcho.

Within minutes, a middle-aged man comes and sits next to me. He takes my wrist and repeats the same procedure. Total exam time: ten minutes or less. He tells me my heart is fine, that I have normal blood pressure, no diabetes, and no heart disease. Without using any instruments, he gathers all this information just from checking my wrists, palms, eyes, fingernails, and tongue. Managed care would love it over here. He hands me a list of thirty herbs with explanations of what they can cure. Every ailment known to humankind is on this list, and it looks a bit like a Chinese menu. He suggests I take number nine, called Bu Ma La, which is indicated for everything from migraines, anger, and worry to sitting uncomfortably, back pain, and something called obnubilation. Yes, this is a real word. If you're curious, check it out online. Hint: it fits in with my entire saga in the Himalayas and has to do with a mental condition. His prescription: take two tablets twice a day for three months and I will be cured of migraines. The pills cost a pittance. This kind of cure would put our Big Pharma out of business. I'm tempted but decide to skip the one from column a, one from column b cure.

Back in my room, all I want to do is climb into bed. Beat and feeling congested, my migraine envelops me. I have one migraine pill left. I decide to save it until I can't stand the pain anymore. Perhaps I should have purchased the Bu Ma La after all, but my skepticism kept my hands in my pockets.

Lying down with a wet cloth on my forehead, I let my mind wander. Are Tibetans with their medicinal herbs, calendar, and star charts any healthier than we are? Their system seems less stressful, with no need for appointments or long waits to see a doctor. Within minutes I was graciously greeted by a doctor, given an exam and diagnosis, and offered treatment on the spot. Compared to the typical 9 A.M. appointment where you sit in a waiting room full of sick people flipping through uninteresting, outdated magazines because the doctor is running late. When asked, the receptionist promises it will only be a few more minutes. Relieved, you return to your seat. Thirty minutes later you sigh in defeat and, if you're anything like me, walk out the door praying that whatever is ailing you can be taken care of at the local CVS.

CHAPTER FORTY-ONE

Leaving the squat behind

May 24, Potala Palace, Lhasa

I'm still feeling poorly but muster enough strength for a tour of the Potala Palace. After slipping into my elephant wash attire of jeans and a shirt, I put on a hat. I just don't have the energy for my whole fashionista routine.

The palace overlooks Lhasa and can be seen for miles from all directions. Once the winter home of the Dalai Lama, it's considered the largest and highest palace in the world and was converted into a museum by the Chinese government. Perched 1,000 feet up on Red Hill, it stands approximately 355 feet tall and is a little more than 1,000 feet wide. With 1,000 rooms, 10,000 shrines, and 200,000 statues, it is divided into two parts: the Red Palace in the center and the White Palace that surrounds it.

It is staggering in size and beyond imagination. Looking like a fortress with alternating red and white walls, it's capped by a striking golden roof.

Sherab tells me that visits are restricted to one hour, but adds that there is no real way for them to monitor so many people. It will take a couple of hours to climb the winding staircase and go through the palace. He hands me my ticket and opts not to join me—his standard routine. I don't think this is how a tour guide is supposed to operate.

Once inside the gate, I face a wide, stone staircase of 432 steps that climbs 1,000 feet before I must work my way back down. My shoes are not made for this exhausting trek, and I'm still in the throes of a full-blown migraine and possibly the beginning of a sinus infection. The altitude isn't helping either. Every few steps I sit down and catch my breath. My heart beating hard, I notice that most of the tourists are equally distressed. Everyone is huffing and puffing and sitting down as often as I do. I want to yell, "Anyone having fun yet?" but think better of it when a weathered old pilgrim, bent over her cane, walks slowly past me. If she can do it, so can I, no further complaints.

When I reach the top, I lean over the massive stone wall and take in the view of Lhasa, its fields and villages, the Jokhang Monastery, and the surrounding mountains. As a young boy, the Dalai Lama would stand here for hours peering through a telescope observing his people and wondering what it was like down there among them.

Turning to go inside, I'm unsure where to begin without a guide so I join a group that is just starting its tour of the Red Palace. The guide explains that there are many levels, galleries, and narrow winding passages. We will see statues, ancient artifacts, chapels, the monk's assembly hall, and libraries containing Buddhist scriptures. Of importance are the elaborate Tibetan tombs of eight Dalai Lamas.

I tag along, listening to the guide as he describes the tomb of the fifth Dalai Lama. Located in the west part of the palace, his enormous pyramid is five stories high and covered in gold inlaid with diamonds, pearls, turquoise, agate, and coral. The pyramid of the thirteenth Dalai Lama is a mere 14 feet high but is emblazoned with 100,000 diamonds and pearls.

Every room in the Red Palace is decorated with exquisite murals. Some are drawn with gold, silver, crushed diamonds, and precious stones, and depict Tibetan's history and culture.

Next we enter a shrine with jeweled, three-dimensional mandalas. Breathtaking, the first one is made of gold and copper and is almost 12 feet wide and high. The monetary and spiritual fortunes that lie within these walls is mind-blowing.

As in all the temples I've visited, there are many pilgrims moving among the chapels. As they present their offerings, they touch their foreheads to the feet of the statues of past Dalai Lamas, their thrones, and anything else considered sacred.

As we walk to the White Palace, the guide tells us it is seven stories high and contains courtyards, temples, offices, the seminary for training Tibetan government officials, the printing house, and the Dalai Lama's former winter home.

We follow her to the fourth floor and the Buddhist hall—a massive room where many major religious and political activities occurred, including the formal enthronement ceremony for the current Dalai Lama at age fifteen.

The last stop worth mentioning is on the roof, where a bright-yellow door leads to the Dalai Lama's living quarters. Called Sunlight Hall, it was named for a full-length window on the south side where the sun pours in all day.

With so much to experience, it is impossible—even with the detailed narration of the guide—to do it justice. And because cameras are forbidden, I must rely on my memory alone. One thing I have no difficulty remembering is the devotion of the Tibetan people to Potala.

Chinese soldiers patrol the inside of the palace, and there are surveillance cameras everywhere. As I mentioned earlier, Chinese law doesn't allow any mention of the current Dalai Lama, even though the tour includes his former chambers. In 2015, a statute was passed by the legislature of southwest China's Tibet Autonomous Region that protects Potala Palace with clear articles on the planning, administration, research, and protection of the structure to preserve its integrity and surroundings.

After meeting up with my inattentive guide, I'm scheduled to visit the Dalai Lama's summer palace, but I decide to go back to my hotel to rest and try to get a good night's sleep. I must get up early for an 8 A.M. flight to Nepal where I have a layover of several hours before I start my journey home. I'll take all my memories with me, but one thing I will gladly say good-bye to: the squat!

CHAPTER FORTY-TWO

A fast track to heaven: the Buddhist way

May 25, Lhasa airport

I'm repacking Big Red, a most symbolic activity. I don't care what it looks like anymore: outfits balled up and stuffed in with squashed hats, a multitude of pills floating around, and dirty underwear. I don't give a damn that my possessions are in total disarray. Its sad condition reflects my personal state. I've been in the same clothes for two days, and sport no makeup and disheveled hair. To eliminate any concerns about how I look to any farmer or monk I might encounter on my trek home, I plunk my straw hat with the black ribbon on my bedraggled hair and don my shades. I'm traveling incognito, and it's a relief.

Before I zip up Red, I decide to jettison a few things: my first souvenir: the Thai t-shirt I bought in downtown Bangkok; four rather heavy travel books still flagged and highlighted; and my stacks of laminated index cards full of instructions and reminders. Some other things I'm delighted to leave behind: pit toilets, taking a bath with an elephant, squatting with a goat, and staring at a plate full of penises. It's not an authentic *trip of a lifetime* if one doesn't face these experiences with no warning. I write a short note that warns travelers against packing curling irons, Waterpiks, hair dryers, white noise machines, or scads of delicate, fashionable clothing and tape it to one of the travel guides. I'm hoping the travel guides, along with my informative note, make their way back to the US and into the hands of anyone insane enough to follow my path down the rabbit hole. Could there possibly be an obsessive-compulsive kindred spirit out there?

On the way to the airport, I experience my final views of Tibet. I see a man in his yard, brushing his teeth and spitting into a pot. I've become accustomed to people tending to bodily functions in the great outdoors. I see drawings of white-painted ladders on the sides of the mountains meant to assist a person's spirit in its ascent to heaven when the body is dead. Some ladders have just two rungs, some have many more. Sherab tells me there are no rules to follow, no set number of rungs; it's however you feel. No questions, no rules, no confessions. What a beautiful and comforting belief. Would anything other than graffiti appear on the hillsides in the West? How I love this religion.

We pass several Buddha images painted on the rocks, including Nietang Buddha, the biggest stone statue engraved on a Tibetan cliff and painted more than 1,100 years ago. The colorful seated Buddha is about 32 feet high and 26 feet wide and can be seen clearly from several miles away. Apparently, I missed it on my way in, but at least I get a glimpse as I leave.

May 25, back at Niti's place in Kathmandu, Nepal

My flight to Nepal is uneventful, though the struggle with Big Red is the same, even in her lightened state. I successfully make my way through another round of swine flu checkpoints and am met by the tour operator. Once again, the sights, sounds, and smells of Kathmandu assault my senses.

I sit in Niti's garden awaiting my driver to another airport, where I will catch my flight back to Bangkok. Ram Hari has taken on the task of hauling Big Red to the garden. He doesn't say anything, but I can tell the stuff I left behind hasn't made much of a dent in Red's weight. Those clothes and shoes, enough for a dozen travelers for a month, are the culprits now. I've approached this the same way as losing weight: not a crash diet but with baby steps over time. That said, give me a few more weeks here and Big Red would be a lot lighter. Maybe I'll retire her altogether and opt for a junior version—a preventative measure in case I weaken.

I'm anxious to get home. I miss Ron, my family and friends. I miss my home and of course, I miss my pearly white porcelain toilets in four fully equipped bathrooms. Sitting in this picturesque garden gives me a few moments to collect my thoughts and reflect on my experiences. The ones that will stay with me the longest are the time spent with the farmers, nomads, and locals in all three kingdoms. I will never forget the richness of each kingdom's culture, born of devotion to their faith and spiritual beliefs. I leave here with a memory of a people who offer the true gift of compassion for all sentient beings, with a welcome invitation into their hearts, homes, and temples.

Last, but not least, I'm truly struck by how their daily lives are filled with backbreaking work, with lots of sweat but no tears, and their hand-built homes, some straight out of the earth. They were born into a world that embraces whatever shows up with few, if any, questions or doubts. Part of me wishes I could be more open to whatever walks through my door—family dogs included.

May 26, Novotel Hotel, Bangkok

Waiting in the Kathmandu airport for my flight to Bangkok, I feel sicker by the minute. Coughing and sneezing up a storm, I'm worried about making it through the swine flu checkpoints. Will I be whisked away and quarantined indefinitely, missing my flight home? I feel warmer than usual. Making sure no one is looking (as if I am doing something illegal), I discreetly pull out my thermometer and take my axillary temperature every thirty minutes to be sure I don't have a fever.

This isn't my only concern. Once in flight, the cabin pressure is having a field day with my ears. By the time I get off the plane, I can't hear a thing. Losing one of your senses is frightening enough, but it's worse when it happens in a foreign place. I'm heading for a ten on the anxiety scale as I attempt to navigate the airport. I have no idea where baggage claim is, so I ask for directions. My voice and the agent's sound like we're talking underwater.

Unable to understand a thing, I keep asking the same question over and over, "Where is baggage claim?" The agent gets impatient as the line behind me lengthens. I can't understand what he's saying, but I sure as hell can read his facial expression: step aside lady, you're holding up the line. It seems I've been in this position before. Does the first-class check-in at JFK ring a bell?

I cup my hands over my ears as I try to demonstrate that I can't hear because my ears are blocked. The agent looks at me strangely and dismisses me. Turning, I look pleadingly at the traveler next to me, but his look suggests he thinks I must be crazy. Frustrated, I get out of line, find a piece of paper, and write on it. I hold up my note to a maintenance man. It reads in big block letters: I'M LOST AND I CAN'T HEAR. PLEASE TAKE ME TO BAGGAGE CLAIM. No questions asked, he takes me right where I need to go.

Just after midnight, I arrive at the Novotel Hotel in Bangkok—one of the most beautiful hotels I have ever stayed in. However, my plan for a quiet night is out when my ears let loose with horrendous pain. I lay my head on the pillow wistfully, knowing that in a matter of hours I will begin my long flight home.

11:30 A.M., Boston, arrival

As I come off the escalator, Ron greets me with a hug and a kiss. He is relieved I am home safe and sound. We walk to baggage claim, and I'm brought full circle as I watch Big Red come around on the carousel. Ron lifts her. The expression on his face says it all. "Way too heavy, Ellie." An all-too-familiar ring.

CHAPTER FORTY-THREE

"Wherever you go, there you are." Jon Kabat-Zinn

My family and friends ask if my *trip of a lifetime* was all I'd hoped it would be. Interesting question. I had so many amazing experiences, but between my ridiculous suitcase full of material trappings and my values and expectations in full-on mode, I had set the stage for an equal amount of frustration and fatigue. There's a clear correlation between the title of Kabat-Zinn's book and my Big Red fiasco. Initially a trip for external exploration, going to the Himalayas evolved into a spiritual journey of self-inquiry and soul-searching. I learned a lot about myself over the course of 15,000 miles, and by all accounts my best teacher was Big Red. Every step of the way, she kept trying to tell me something.

Seeing others struggle to lift her made me painfully aware that my obsessive-compulsive nature, and rigid concept of how life should be, does not line up with Buddhist philosophy.

Traveling in a land where simplicity reigns, Big Red was a symbol of how attached I am to what matters least. With each opening and closing, each lift and drag, I was more preoccupied with how to hang on to my must-haves instead of being in the moment. I almost lost sight of the meaning of my journey.

Venturing into the unknown was not the perfect journey that I'd imagined. Despite months of planning, I was frequently pushed off course by my perfectionism. From the moment I attempted to book my first round of flights, I was confronted with obstacles at every turn. In the face of my intense vanity and obsessions, I learned a profound lesson or two from the people and cultures I encountered. Their simple lifestyle leaves no time for anything more than what is necessary. Everything is linked to their spirituality. Compassion, love, and respect for all sentient beings is ingrained in them. Western dress, entertainment, food, and technology has begun to infiltrate the landlocked kingdoms of the Himalayas. Embraced by the younger generation, it remains to be seen if these changes will erode or destroy their cultures. For now, there seems to be a commitment to preserving the old while living in concert with the new.

Ian Zimmerman—an experimental psychologist who studies consumer behavior—once said, "True happiness rarely lies at the bottom of a shopping bag." But is it an all-or-nothing proposition? Or can you have what you want yet somehow live above it? Will I ever be able to leave behind the adornments of the Western world in my search for a simpler way of being? Where will my peace, contentment, and happiness come from? If and when I make the discovery, the bigger question may be whether I have the spiritual and emotional mettle to make the necessary changes. Time will tell.

EPILOGUE

"If there is no struggle, there is no progress."
~Frederick Douglass

Seven years later

When I returned with a suitcase still tipping the scale at 95 pounds, I knew I had some work to do if I wanted to change my off-the-wall neurotic lifestyle. Putting into action what I learned from Big Red was frustrating. Freeing myself from the things I coveted and inflexible routines was difficult. Clothes were bagged as I haggled with my inner self: Keep it? Don't keep it? Debates played out in my head when asked to forego my day's agenda and do something spontaneous. But the biggest challenge was letting go of the drive for perfection that continued to leave its mark on every facet of my life. Attempts to resist the need to be put together or accepting that there is no such thing as maintaining a perfect-all-white inner sanctum caused me angst. But experience told me no matter how high I aimed, perfection was a moving target. My trip and frequent visits from those four-legged animals was the proof.

Mind sets are hard to break because they are deeply embedded in our psyche. Did I want to own *stuff* or have *it* own me? Did I need to impress friends and family to validate my self-worth? The answer was a resounding no. I had to do more than rearrange the scenery. To bring about meaningful change for a simpler, more authentic way of being, my core beliefs had to be altered.

I needed to start unpacking the workings of my thoughts to find a reliable happiness. It started with keeping control of the compulsions that threaten to hijack my efforts. Every morning, I set daily goals to recognize self-limiting behaviors that are unhealthy and choose wiser responses.

I was put to the test with a Christmas present from Ron, a smaller version of Big Red. Preparing to pack for a lengthy trip to Europe, Little Red stood in the corner. Piled on the bed were a host of nonessentials: an array of drugstore products, cosmetics, and vanity items, plus the overkill of electronics, outfits, shoes, and bottles of supplements. It was déjà vu. I couldn't possibly fit it all in that suitcase. As the image of her larger sister flashed before me, Ron entered the room, sensed my dilemma, and shook his head. "Really, Ellie?" I paused and listened to the power of my inner voice: *You are at a crossroad.*

Checking in at the airport, a familiar scene unfolded. Next to me, a woman on all fours was frantically pulling things out of her suitcase to lighten *her* load. It was a comfort knowing I wasn't alone in my craziness. Once Little Red was weighed in and on her way, I wanted to say, "I've been there. Can I give you some advice?" But if she were anything like me, she'd need to learn it the hard way.

I'm less trapped in my old ways of thinking. Errands and outings are often makeup-free. Obsessive aisle routines during supermarket runs have been eliminated. I manage to shop at different stores with little or no stress. Invitations to impromptu outings and dinners are more readily accepted. Empty clothes hangers have equal billing with full ones in my closets. Bathrooms still sparkle, but cobwebs and dust bunnies have found new homes. Doggy accidents remain a source of irritation, but they are no longer followed by an explosion of profanities.

A complete abandonment of my Western ways will never happen. I won't wake up one morning and decide peace and contentment will be guaranteed by moving to a smaller dwelling. As long as I strive to make wholesome choices, ones that create balance and keep me moving in the right direction, it's enough. Oh, and the status of Big Red—officially retired!

The path to peace and tranquility has not been a straight one. It's been a mix of highs and lows, twists and turns, and some backtracking. There are still times when I carry way too much baggage—material *and* emotional. I sometimes search for happiness in all the wrong places, but I punish myself less. On days when I don't move with the grace of Buddha, I work hard to reside in my true nature. Some days I catch the joy by lightening my load, even if just a little. I'm grateful to Big Red for revealing my shortcomings in a new light. She made me aware of how my suffering is often caused by my tight grip on perfection and a desire for more.

As far back as I can remember, my life has been focused on self-improvement in mind, body, and spirit. It is *the* single most important aspect of my life. In the words of Socrates, "The unexamined life is not worth living." I'm a work in progress; there is no race to the finish line. I struggle less, breathe more, and practice staying in the moment. I am in the middle of my story, and what I've learned so far is this: if I want to achieve the wisdom of the Buddha, I must travel light—in more ways than one!

The quote on my refrigerator sums it up. "Finish each day and be done with it. You have done what you could. Some blunders and absurdities no doubt crept in; forget them as soon as you can. Tomorrow is a new day. You shall begin it serenely and with too high a spirit to be encumbered with your old nonsense." ~ Ralph Waldo Emerson.

Namaste,

Ellie

NOTES ALONG THE WAY

This book evolved from my Trip of a Lifetime blog. Posting almost daily during my journey, I started it for my family and friends, but it quickly generated a following of loyal readers in the US, Europe, and Asia. Encouraging and forthright, their comments about my struggles, missteps, and challenges became part of my story; and I would be remiss not to share some of the more memorable entries.

Along with the serious lessons I learned on my journey, I treasure the levity and kindhearted companionship I found through my blog.

Missed flight:

~ How in the world could you possibly miss your connection when you were five feet from the boarding ramp?

~ Oh Lord, Mom. Please pay attention. You are in a foreign country!

~ Ellie, breathe. There is a higher spirit guiding you. But I must reiterate Michele's comments: "For God's sake pay attention and help out the guide!"

~ Think of the fun and wonderful sites you will see in Bhutan— that is, if you ever get there; remember, this is what you always wanted to do or at least what you are trying to do!

All-night shopping in Bangkok:

~ Were you really shopping with a strange man at midnight for *underwear?* Part of the itinerary?

~ So your first purchases were a Thai t-shirt and some underwear. Fabulous! How are those new briefs treating you?

~ I guess you won't have to worry about your big red suitcase for a while. Just think, when you get your red monk's robes you won't need underwear.

Pit toilets and squatter's anxiety:

~ OK, cuzz... since you are having this obsession about "going" in a hole out in the open, here is my advice. Wear pants with elastic and a skirt over the pants. Just pull down and do the deed. Keep separate your emotions from the basic act, pretend you have already successfully done it once, and go from there. Buddha says, "It is the feelings generated by the thoughts we have that are the messengers." So drop the emotion, drop your pants, do the deed, and just get on with it!

~ Listen, Mom, when you gotta go, you gotta go. There aren't going to be any luxuries on this vacation. If you wanna chant like the monks you're gonna have to crap like the monks! Twirl those mala beads, say "Om" a few times, and let it allllll out! Keep smiling and remember "you're in the "happy place" now.

~ Oh, Ellie, you are definitely on an adventure. Just be careful nothing jumps out of a hole and bites you in the ass!

~ Hey Ellie, we're so enjoying your trip! Don't let the bathroom thing get in the way of your fun—just do as the Romans do and shit in the damn hole! That's my advice!

~ Oh Ellie, just go, otherwise you're gonna end up with a urinary tract infection, or worse a bowel obstruction and need a colostomy performed in a foreign country. Go, be one with nature! You'll be back home to use your pearly white porcelain toilet before you know it and you will be even more grateful for your wonderful life. Hope everything comes out okay. (Hint!)

~ Hi Ellie. My advice on the great outdoors toilet situation is to concentrate on all the women all over the world who through the ages have squatted not only for elimination but childbirth. You will really be the ultimate recycler. Al Gore will be proud of you for not wasting water. It will be a lesson in humility.

~ Wooden sticks instead of toilet paper, really? My comment will be brief. "OUCH!"

Welcome to paradise and the mighty jungle:

~ Mom, take my advice. You need to wake up and see you are not of the Western world or in the Western world. Maybe then your trip of a lifetime will really begin!

~ No toilets and now no electricity! Thank you very much for not inviting me along on your trip of a lifetime.

~ Ellie, you're in the jungle. Did you expect wine and roses?

~ Riding an elephant solo? Keep reminding us of all the reasons why no one joined you on… what did you call it?—the "trip of a lifetime"?

~ Excuse me, but how much did you pay to see "rhino" shit or any other of kind of shit for that matter?

~ What kind of person hates insects yet goes into the jungle? Ellie, only Ellie.

~ Again we ask you. You paid to do what? Wash an elephant? Be bathed by an elephant???

~ Stepping in shit, looking at shit (rhino)—I haven't read this in any travel guide. Maybe you should write one of your own—these are your words: "Things you can expect not to experience: real toilets, exotic animals, electricity, luxury getaways, and so much more. What you will experience: pit toilets, deadly mosquitoes, unmanned elephant rides, fire hazard rooms, sleeping with the enemy (insects and geckos) and so much more."

~ Your claim to fame can now be said that you not only bathed with an elephant, but you crapped with a goat. Who can beat that?

The clothing and what's in the suitcase:

~ You look great on that donkey and the pictures are worth the wait. But proper attire would certainly be more suitable for trekking up 10,000 feet.

~ Have you forgotten where you are? Like the jungle. Don't you have at least one article of clothing that is practical in that big red suitcase?

Big Red—too much stuff; not the right stuff:

~ Ellie, maybe if you dump the curling iron, the white noise machine, several of those inappropriate outfits and shoes, just maybe you won't break your neck lifting, dragging, and pushing the big red suitcase around. Just a thought!

~ At your next temple visit let your Waterpik be an offering to the Buddha. He would be so proud of you!

~ Do not cart that half gallon of mosquito repellent and all those cans of Deet spray in that damned big red suitcase another mile. Take a cue from your successful squat: "Let it go"—and then some!

~ How about getting rid of those 484 vitamins you aren't taking?

Why there?

~ If anyone needs more proof as to why Ellie went alone on this trip of a lifetime think about the list that continues to get longer every day: toilet pits, nonstop barking dogs, no electricity, the dengue and the swine flu.... No doubt I'm missing some things, but knowing Ellie by now, I'm sure there's more to come.

~ Slabs of meat with flies a plenty? Say no more, Ellie, say no more!

~ Chinese menu, and medicine for what ails you: Okay Ellie, this is the last straw. Stewed sheep's head, fish bladder and pork uterus. Stick to the cereal and milk.

~ I second that especially when it comes to penis and testicle pu pu platters.

~ What better way to serve those beastly parts but on a plate!

~ What could Rachael Ray do in 30 minutes with those ingredients?

~ So penis is good for your complexion. I wonder how they would package penis in a jar for your skin? What do you think the logo would look like?

~ The number nine you say is called "Bu Ma La" and cures everything from migraines to something called obnubilation. It sounds obscene, which seems to fit in with everything else you have done and seen.

~ Bu ma *what*? Have you seen or done anything close to normal during this trip? I don't think so.

The Mad Monk's thunderbolt:

~ Was that really a painting of a big fat penis with hairy testicles tied with a bow painted on a wall on your blog?

~ Ooh! That can't be a picture of what I think it is on that wall. Of course it is! Where else would you see such a sight?

~ Wow, what a picture of the "flaming thunderbolt." Hey that gives me an idea for the Yankee swap at Christmas, Aunt Ellie. So how about bringing a few samples home?

~ Great stocking stuffers, Mom

~ Mom, you have been blessed by a holy man and now a monk who held a wooden penis over your head. This is one religion I would have remained actively involved in.

~ Reason for traveling with Ellie: Cannabis, Cannabis, Cannabis!

Final blog comment:

~ Your family and friends all say, "Do not think of staying one more day. Heavy or not, just drag that big ass red monster home. We cannot survive another blog about this trip."

ACKNOWLEDGMENTS

I would like to express my deepest appreciation to two individuals:

- MaryChris Bradley, a thirty-five year veteran of the book industry, award-winning book publisher, and founder of Buddhapuss Ink.

- Janet Sadler, editor, who pored over the words, chapters, and offered comments and advice that contributed a richness to my story.

Also, my thanks to:

- Robert Charles of East Longmeadow, an award-winning photographer, who helped create a strong cover image that portrayed the spirit and essence of *Big Red*.

- Asian Pacific Adventures, for planning an incredible trip of a lifetime.

And finally, I will be forever grateful to the Himalayan people who welcomed me into their homes and hearts, and allowed me to experience a lifestyle and culture wholly influenced by their spiritual beliefs.

63578756R00148

Made in the USA
Middletown, DE
03 February 2018